THEY SAID NO TO WAR

ROBERT LIVINGSTON

Paperback: 978-1-958381-44-1
eBook: 978-1-958381-45-8
Library of Congress Control Number: 2022916922

This is a work of nonfiction.

SWEETSPIRE **LITERATURE**
——— MANAGEMENT ———

This book is dedicated to my friends and family... Thanks for being there.

TABLE OF CONTENTS

INTRODUCTION

The decision to go to war is the most momentous action an American president can take. Sending young men and women into combat weighs heavily on the Commander in Chief, as it does on the Congress, which must authorize war. The framers of the Constitution understood the necessity of creating this division of power in order to restrain the chief executive's war powers. Necessarily a degree of tension was expected, even encouraged between the two branches of government. This view held sway in order to foster debate and discussion before entering a war. America's colonial experience under British rule, and the history of European conflicts also weighed heavily on those meeting in Philadelphia in 1787. Years later Abraham Lincoln summed up their concerns:

> *Kings had always been involving and impoverishing their people into wars, pretending generally, if not always, that the good of the people was the object. This our Constitutional Convention understood to be the most oppressive of all Kingly oppressions and they resolved to so frame the Constitution that no one man should hold the power to bring on an oppressive war.*

It was always accepted that objectives of America's foreign policy would evolve over time in response to a changing world. It was assumed that in time certain fundamental principles would dominate our foreign policy. For example:

Isolationism: this policy initially meant to keep out of European embroilments. Later it took on other aspects, including non-intervention, different degrees of neutrality, and always an aversion to entangling alliances.

Freedom of the Seas: this policy declared the right of America ships to sail anywhere in the world, even to nations involved in a war. This also meant that our trade with the world was not subject to restraints.

Peaceful Settlement of Dispute: this policy gave primacy to negotiations as a way to arbitrate disputes. Treaties and agreements, where possible, were better than bullets and bombs.

The objectives of these policies were security, prosperity, and peace if at all possible. It was always understood that absolute strict isolationism was never possible, especially when nations went to war. The question was always to what degree would American involvement take, and what would be the nature of that involvement? The two questions have beset every occupant of the White House.

Our wars have always been costly, whether they were fought for avowed noble reasons, or questionable ignoble justifications as shown below:

WAR/YEARS	BATTLE DEATHS	CAUSE
American Revolution 1775-1783	4,435	Freedom and Independence
Mexican War 1846-1848	1,733	Acquisition of the Southwest
Spanish-American War 1898	385	Free Cuba of Spanish Control
World War I 1917-1918	53,409	Make the World Safe for Democracy
World War II 1941-1945	291557	Defeat the Axis Powers
Korean War 1950-1953	3,739	Cold War Confrontation
Vietnam War 1964-1975	47,434	Testing the Domino Theory
Desert Shield/Storm 1990 -1991	148	Invading Iraq

The cause of each war was always open to interpretation and, therefore, has led to endless debate. The battle death figures shown do not include non-battlefield deaths, or civilian fatalities. Nor do they include American Civil War battle deaths, which were unimaginable and a prologue for World War I. The Confederacy lost 258,000. The Union dead totaled 360,222. Finally, these statistics do not include the wounded, either in body or mind.

It is true that most people abhor war, yet war still resonates with an appeal. It is romanticized. Heroics are celebrated Honors are awarded for duty and service. Sacrifice is memorialized. Citizens recall marching bands and the flag flyting gloriously in the air as they sang patriotic lyrics, and later glorified battles and victories. They do not always recall the words of Erich Maria Remarque's classic *All Quiet on the Western Front* written after World War I. A young German soldier confesses to the heavens:

> *Yet I know nothing of life but despair, death, fear...I see how peoples are set against one another, and in silence, unknowingly, foolishly, obediently, innocently slay one another.*

And continuing:

We see soldiers run with their two feet cut off, they stagger on their splintered stumps into the next shell-hole; a lance-corporal crawls a mile and a half on his hands dragging his smashed knee after him; another goes to the dressing station and over his clasped hands bulge his intestines; we see men without mouths, without jaws...

Still, countries go to war supported by applauding citizens. Some do so out of ignorance or a lack of understanding. Some are susceptible to wild emotions and self-deception. Others are galvanized by fear and anger, and alleged grievances or assumed injuries. Some support war and even want to participate. What motivates them? Boredom sometimes moves them. Others may simply crave excitement. Many have a naïve view of war and glory. Some many simply need an outlet for their angers.

Whatever their reasons for going to war, countries always feel they are in the right. They find endless justifications for doing so. This, some argue, is the root cause of war. The former Secretary General of the U.N., Dag Hammarskjold, once aptly said:

We are on dangerous ground if we believe that any nation has a monopoly on rightness.

This brings us to a difficult question. Is war inevitable? If answered in the affirmative, then what is the role and responsibility of political leaders? Are our leaders helpless? Is the situation hopeless? If answered in the negative then wars are to a large extent a matter of choice usually related to either maintaining the existing status quo or attempting to upend it. The Romans tried to fight off the barbarians. The Confederacy sought to end a relationship with Washington. The Cold War was a battle of national wills, but also a struggle between competing economic systems and the place, philosophically speaking, of the citizen. Which was more important, individualism or the collective approach to bringing about social justice?

We could also ask if leaders are trapped by the decisions of their predecessors? Are leaders held hostage to contemporary political events, meaning an upcoming election? Are leaders fastened to their own prejudices and the needs of their own emotional egos, all of which can affect their decisions? Causation is difficult to ascribe here when it comes to determining why decisions are made to go to war. The best we can say is that many forces influence our leaders and their decisions. The one thing we cannot say is this; historical forces beyond our control are working themselves out. This is akin to saying "it's all in God's hands." This is the acceptance of the inevitable. This view must be rejected. As former President John F. Kennedy said:

> *Our problems are man-made. Therefore, they can be solved by man... No problem of human destiny is beyond human beings. Man's reason and spirit have often solved the seemingly unsolvable --- and we believe they can do it again.*

Whenever our nation goes to war there are always those who dissent. In the frenzy of war lust and national anger their voices are usually shunted aside as unpatriotic, misguided, or somehow aiding a foe. Almost always the response to dissent is vicious and immediate, highly emotional and often irrational. Seldom are the salient points of debate discussed on their merits.

What follows is the story of seven very special people. Each of them voted against going to war. What did they have in common? First, each had strong convictions against war? They all had a pacifist streak that restrained them from impetuous, short-term decision-making when it came to authorizing a war resolution. Second, all had inquisitive minds that provoked troubling questions. Details and hard intelligence information was important to them. Third, they were all willing to act on the basis of principle. They were all willing to put aside political pragmatism and personal ambitions. On the issue of war they were not poll-driven. Fourth, they all had a maverick streak to them. Being in the minority was nothing new for them. They were used to taking heat from their colleagues. Standing up to others, whether in Congress or the White House, was a necessity determined by their individual moral compass. Beyond that, when necessary they were willing to defy their own constituents and risk future defeat at the polls. Fifth, they always understood how easy it was to get into a war and how difficult it was to end one. Implications, ramifications, and unintended consequences were always of concern to them. Sixth, all fervently believed in social justice and domestic policies to improve the lot of the common man. All feared that war would devastate that effort. They were unwilling to see that occur.

Who were the seven? In 1915 William Jennings Bryan resigned as Secretary of State. He would no longer accede to the policies of President Woodrow Wilson. Bryan felt those policies would soon entangle America in the European conflict, which had begun a year earlier. The war press of that day hurled unrelenting criticism at a man who had run unsuccessfully three times for the White House as a Democrat. Departing the Wilson Cabinet all but ended his political career.

WILLIAM JENNNINGS BRYAN

In 1917 President Wilson asked for a Declaration of War against Germany and her allies. In the Senate, George Norris of Nebraska and Robert LaFollette, Sr. of Wisconsin voted no. Experienced and principled and with a stubborn streak, they resisted the war fever that overtook the country. They were not pacifists. They understood that war was sometimes a necessity. No nation can turn away from a direct attack. And that was the problem for them. The United States had not been attacked. No German troops were assaulting the country.

GEORGE NORRIS   ROBERT LAFOLLETTE

In the House of Representatives the only woman in Congress and the first woman elected to Congress, Jeannette Rankin, voted against war.

JEANNETTE RANKIN

On the day she was sworn in to represent Montana in the House of Representatives her first vote would decide if America went to war. Discarding all the pragmatic advice to consider her political future, she voted for peace. Twenty-five years later during a second term in the House, she would vote against war following the attack on Pearl Harbor. That objection was the only dissenting vote in the Congress on December 8, 1941.

In the 1960's two members of the Senate voted against what would be called the Tonkin Gulf Resolution. They were Wayne Morse of Oregon and Ernest Gruening of Alaska.

WAYNE MORSE   ERNEST GRUENING

They were fervently opposed to President Lyndon Johnson's request to send more troops to Southeast Asia. They did not want the United States involved in the civil war raging in Vietnam. They feared the War Resolution gave too much power to the White House and that could lead to an endless conflict. They refused to accept the so-called Domino Theory, which maintained the loss of one country would lead to other countries falling under communist control in Asia.

In more recent times only one member of the House of Representatives voted against President George Bush's War Resolution to fight in Afghanistan. Her name was Barbara Lee. She represented the people of Oakland, California and Alameda County. She was unwilling to give the President a "blank check" to fight Islamic terrorism. In the difficult days after the bombing of the Twin Towers in New York City she was a lone voice in the

House, a black woman standing against the frenzy for revenge. As in the case of those already mentioned, she was pilloried for taking an unpopular stance.

BARBARA LEE

All of these people exemplified political courage under fire in their willingness to dissent. Their stories are worth knowing.

BOOK 1

WAR

On Sunday, June 28, 1914, the Archduke Franz Ferdinand of Austria was assassinated along with his wife, Sophie. The Archduke was heir to the Austro-Hungarian throne. The royal couple was killed in the town of Sarajevo in the provincial capital of Bosnia. The killer was a young student and Serbian nationalist. His name was Gavailo Princip. The political objective of the assassination was to create an independent Bosnia free of Vienna's control, and to establish a South Slav State. Princip and others involved in the plot were caught by the police and later sentenced to various punishments, including death. That should have been the end of the incident. It wasn't.

Almost a month later the civilized nations of Europe proceeded to go to war. An alliance system, years in the making, came into play and countries drifted headlong over an abyss. The alliance system divided Europe into warring camps. The Central Powers or Triple Alliance was composed of Germany, Austria-Hungary, and the Ottoman Empire. The Triple Entente (later called the Allies) included, Great Britain, France, and Russia. Later Japan and Italy would join the Entente. The purpose of the alliances was to provide mutual cooperation and defense. No country wanted to be isolated and vulnerable. That meant, of course, that if any country were attacked others in the alliance would come to that country's aid. When Austria-Hungary threatened to attack Serbia, the Russians mobilized against Vienna. In response the Germans did the same to assist their ally. Quickly other countries honored their agreements and by July 28, 1914 the continent marched off to war.

Europeans expected a short war, not one that would last over three years. Their point of reference was the Franco-Prussian War of 1870, which was fought by small, professional armies, and concluded quickly with relatively little loss of life. They did not understand that they were beginning a global war that would be fought in Asia, the Middle East, Africa, and not just the European plain. They did not fully appreciate the killing power of a new weapon, the machine gun. They did not think a stalemate, best described as trench warfare, would overtake their best military plans. They could not envision trenches stretching from the English Channel to Switzerland. They had no idea they were embracing a war that would be the deadliest conflict in human history to that time. They could not imagine that 9-million would die in combat, and millions more would be wounded, nor that over 5-million civilians were to also perish from hunger and disease.

Looming over the self-created holocaust was the United States. What would Washington's policy be toward the belligerent nations? Initially, most Americans wanted to keep out of the senseless conflict. The *Chicago Herald* put it this way:

> Peace loving citizens of this country will now rise up and tender a hearty vote of thanks to Columbus for having discovered America.

The *Wabash Plain Dealer* added:

> We never appreciated so keenly as now the foresight exercised by our own forefathers in emigrating from Europe.

The *Literary Digest* stated:

> Our isolated position and freedom from entangling alliances inspire our press with the cheering assurance that we are in no peril of being drawn into the European quarrel.

The general view was that Europe should "stew in its own juices," and that was good advice as long as the pot didn't boil over. At least at the beginning of the war Europe seemed a long way off and the issues involved had little to do with America. The dreadful business came as a surprise to most Americans, "like lightning out of a clear sky," according to our Ambassador to Great Britain, Walter Hines Page.

President Woodrow Wilson stated early on that, "the effect of the war upon the United States will depend upon what Americans citizens say and do."

Every man who really loves America will act and speak in the true spirit of neutrality, which is the spirit of impartiality and fairness, and friendliness to all concerned.

The President summarized his policy as such: "The United States must be neutral in fact as well as in name during the days that are to try men's souls."

The President understood that America was a hyphenated nation. In 1914 the population was approximately 92-million. Of that total 33-million were foreign born. Eleven million were from Germany and central Europe. Over 5-million were from Ireland. That being the case Wilson argued "Americans must be neutral since otherwise our mixed population would wage war on each other."

The question, of course, was how to implement neutrality in a "fair and impartial manner?" As the European war progressed this question became both more complicated and difficult. On the one side was the traditional American policy of freedom of the seas. Added to this was the right of individual Americans to enjoy unrestricted travel. If the British and Germans in particular resorted to war zones at sea and stopped or sank American ships, what would this mean? Certainly businesses had the legal right to trade with all nations. Did this include munitions? Did this include food and medicine? Banks and private individuals had the right to loan funds to belligerents in both alliances, and to extend enormous credits. Depending on how the war went, how would such funds be repaid? At what point would these activities entangle the country in the European folly?

Over the ensuing years American public opinion changed from the strictest neutrality to a full-fledged involvement. There were many reasons for this, all summarized by a few words penned by Robert Underwood Johnson"

Forget us, God, if we forget
The sacred sword of Lafayette!

On April 2, 1917 President Woodrow Wilson asked Congress to approve a declaration of war against Germany and her allies. As expected a majority of the Senate and House of Representatives voted two days later for war. Three individuals, however, voted "no." In doing so, and in abiding by their convictions, they jeopardized their political careers and were besieged by scorn and unrelenting criticism. One was a Senator from Nebraska, George William Norris. Another Senator was from Wisconsin, Robert Marion LaFollette. A third person was the first woman ever elected to the United States Congress, Representative Jeannette Rankin from Montana. Had he been in Congress a fourth politician would have voted against war with Germany. That was William Jennings Bryan. As Secretary of State he had resigned in opposition to President Wilson's policies in 1915, which he felt would lead to war. He also endured criticism for his stance.

The political courage of these four is at the focus of the chapters that follow. But not that alone… What were their hopes and dreams as representatives of the voters? What were their accomplishments as elected officials? Why were they willing to tilt with windmills and withstand the pressure to entangle America in the European War? And, of course, what lessons can we draw today from their courageous stance when it comes to questions of war?

PART I

WILLIAM JENNINGS BRYAN

THERE CAN BE NO SETTLEMENT OF A GREAT CAUSE WITHOUT DISCUSSION, AND PEOPLE WILL NOT DISCUSS A CAUSE UNTIL THEIR ATTENTION IS DRAWN TO IT.

CHAPTER 1

THE REPORTER AND THE DIPLOMA

THE MASON HOTEL – OCTOBER 1915

The Mason was an old-line hotel located at First and Main in a once thriving business section of Washington D.C. Constructed in 1883 by investors in steel and railroads monopolies, it was a temporary residence for the well heeled, including aspiring politician new to the nation's capital and business folks seeking government contracts. Over the years newer and fancier hotels were built in the city leaving the Mason, some thought, a bit long in the tooth, if not shoddy in appearance. Those who frequented the hotel knew, as many already knew, you shouldn't judge a book by its cover, nor a hotel by its outward age.

The Mason provided excellent service by experienced folks who were the very soul of discretion as they quietly went about their business, always attentive to the needs of their patrons. The lobby was wide and inviting with comfortable chairs and a plethora of magazines and newspaper for those idling away the time, or desirous of a quiet place for an intimate conversation. A very large fireplace blazed during the chilling winter months, and multiple fans clung to the ceiling, quietly humming away during the blistering summers. Handheld fans were available for the ladies in particular who enjoyed the personal touch. Cigarettes and cigars were placed in lovely rectangular shaped boxes imported from China. The hotel staff made sure Cuban cigars were plentiful, and the cigarette containers full. Naturally, there was always a wisp of smoke in the air.

A newly installed elevator cranked and squealed as it lifted through the possibilities of one of six floors. A kindly, middle-aged man announced each floor, pointing out to all that their luggage was already in their rooms. Though few knew it, the elevator operator was Jake Fields from Brooklyn. Back in 1898 he had been severely wounded in the famous charge up San Juan Hill in Cuba. Theodore Roosevelt, the bespectacled future president of the United States and fearless leader of the Rough Riders, had personally noted Jake for his courage under fire. A job at the Mason had been his salvation once he was released from the service and a military hospital.

The dining room was functional, not ornate. The mahogany tables seated four with straight chairs nicely padded for the comfort of all, yet stiff enough to discourage guests from excessive lingering. The kitchen staff was small but experienced and competent in its culinary pursuits. While providing for breakfast and mid-day meals, the chefs excelled with three basic menu selections for dinner. Excellent sirloin steaks were always in season from barely heated for those who enjoyed a pink look to their meat, or torched in the name of "well done." All shades in between were possible and provided as requested. Of course, fried chicken was a staple, seasoned by those who would die rather than divulge the secret ingredients involved. Well-baked or fried Atlantic fish was available for others, a delight certainly for good Catholics on Friday. For those who preferred fresh water trout from the local rivers of Virginia and Maryland, that too was provided. The two chefs were from the "Deep South," one from New Orleans, and the other from Galveston, Texas. They made for an interesting duo in the kitchen as their competitive juices ranged far and wide as to which one was king in the kitchen. The patrons, of course, knew little of this.

On June 8, 1915 it was unusually chilly and long coats, woolen scarfs, and tightly worn hats were appropriate. A city taxi brought one such person cloaked in this manner to the Mason. This individual exited the taxi after providing the driver with a generous tip. An on-the-spot bellhop quickly opened the hotel doors. Another youthful bellhop equally as fast on his feet escorted this rather large man with a mane of white hair peeking out from under his hat to Jake's elevator. The man walked across the lobby like some immovable chunk of granite with powerful legs propelling him across the lobby with a hefty stride. The attentive hotel manager acknowledged the man with a slight nod that was reciprocated in kind. Momentarily others glimpsed the man, discerning only a great coat on the move. Forewarned about this man Jake Fields took him to the sixth floor where he departed with a muted "thank you." As he did so Jake thought to himself under his breath, "It really was him and in my elevator."

The man hurried down the narrow corridor to Room 310. It was at the far end of the hall. There he stopped before crisply rapping three times on the door. A few seconds later the door opened and the man entered the room. For the longest moment he stared at the room's occupant. Then …

"Mr. Marty Cohen?"
"Mr. Secretary of State?"

CHAPTER 2

OPENING SALVOS

Marty Cohen gestured to a tall coat rack where his coat already hung, along with his battered old hat. Another coat and hat was added, though of a more recent vintage. Marty again gestured to a comfortable chair and the two men sat down. No words were immediately said as the two men looked at each other. It was obvious that they were sizing up the other; taking stock, if you will of a potential protagonist much like to gladiators in the ancient Coliseum. To an outsider one was tall and strongly built with a barrel chest and great powerful hands that seemed always in motion once words poured from the man. By comparison, the other man seemed small and frail with a body that seemed in perpetual motion, twitching this way and that, even as his eyes darted back and forth. What the two men had in common was an intensity that burned through the night, much like hot rivets fastened to iron and steel. If intellect can be seen or smelled both men were endowed with insightful personalities and steel-trap minds. Little got past them and each appeared able to pounce if necessary to make a point. Physical appearances aside they, as time would show, were shadowy reflections of each other.

"Sir, how should I address you?"
"Mr. Secretary."
"Much too formal."

"WJB."

"Lifeless initials."

"Bryan."

"Pedestrian."

"William Jennings?"

"More colorful."

"But?"

"Perhaps William would suffice?"

"Mr. Cohen, I have heard that you are insufferable. Let's compromise. Refer to me as Mr. Secretary."

"Some compromise!"

"I'm here, am I not, Mr. Cohen?"

"Marty, please. You are here, and that weighs in your favor. I concede."

The abbreviated Introductions were over. It was time to get down to business. Both men knew that."

"Mr. Secretary, one question, please… Why did you agree to meet with me? After all, I'm a known Socialist reporting for newspaper held suspect by the federal government for salacious editorials condemning the selfish breed of those who exploit industrial workers. Many view me as an anarchist, or worse yet, a budding Bolshevik. And not to put too find a point on it I am considered a potentially disloyal commodity, especially if America joins the insanity afflicting Europe. My reporting has, as you know, been highly critical of the Wilson Administration for actions that will lead to war. I have peppered the president and lashed out at his two lackeys, the pompous Colonel House and his obedient servant, Robert Lansing. Both men, I think, are dragging Wilson into the European conflict."

"You have indeed been harsh."

"They favor the Entente. They seek a British/French victory over the Germans. There is no question about that."

"You have not included me in your journalistic jousting."

Marty Cohen gave his guest a sharp eye and them, carefully choosing his words. "You have been stalwart against their ruinous policies, the only real force in the Cabinet acting to that end. My only complaint is that you have not lashed out more forcefully against your colleagues."

"I am constrained."

"Perhaps to a fault."

"You do reach for the jugular."

"Sir, it is who I am and what I do."

"Then I am on guard, Marty."

"Which brings me back to my question; why have you agreed to meet with me?"

"Because of what I will do tomorrow, I must meet with you."

"Tomorrow?"

"I will tender my resignation to President Wilson. I will resign as Secretary of State and leave the Cabinet. By noon tomorrow I will be a private citizen."

Few things startled Marty Cohen. He had seen and heard both the depravity of life and brave effort of others to do the right thing, often against the most difficult odds. Little shocked him anymore. In Europe he observed old and great empires locked in mortal combat, apparently willing to kill a generation of young men in some elusive goal of victory and national security. The statesmen call it war and define themselves as belligerents, implausible words to describe what they are --- savage butchers hoodwinking large populations into a struggle where only death is the victor. Here in the United States

Marty Cohen had witnessed children chained on the assembly line in dangerous factories working through the day for survival wages. He had observed the near slave conditions of black tenant farmers living in the disgrace of a fully segregated society south of the Mason-Dixon Line. He had gone into the wretched coal mines of West Virginia and Kentucky where the sun never shone and toxic air silently killed. He had witnessed the onerous conditions of women working twelve-hour shifts or more in shirt factories where there was little regard for their safety and where fire and locked doors were an ever-present danger. He had walked the crowded slums and seen lifeless unemployed men seeking a hot meal. Still, what Marty Cohen had just heard left him speechless.

"You have reached an impasse with President Wilson?"

"If the president continues to follow his evolving pro-British and French position against Germany, he will soon entrap America in the useless hemorrhage of death and destruction devouring Europe. That I cannot abide."

"Still, why meet with me. Why not the Washington papers or the *New York Times*? Certainly, they could provide greater coverage and deliver this story to more people. My flimsy paper reaches only those already at odds with our exploitive economic system catering to the wealthy at the expense of those born under a different star. Our anti-war position is well known and in stone.

"That is precisely why I sit across from you, Marty."

"Elucidate, please."

The Secretary of State stood, paced around the room before abruptly stopping. Glaring at Marty and perhaps at demons beyond the room, he said, "Do you know what will happen tomorrow after I submit my note of resignation?"

"As you have said, you'll be a private citizen."

"Beyond that?"

"What?"

"The President Woodrow Wilson will accept my resignation with regret."

WOODROW WILSON

"And?"

"Kind words will be thrown in my direction for service to his administration and my many years in government. Colonel Edward House, Wilson's most trusted adviser and unofficial personal envoy to the belligerent countries, will increasingly have the president's ear. Already circumventing the State Department as Wilson's personal envoy to London and Paris, he will continue to do so, favoring American involvement. Robert Lansing, seen as the unofficial Secretary of State, will immediately be offered my position. Already heavily pro-English and supportive of the Entente, he will further that position once Secretary to bring America into the war. He makes no bones about this. Wilson will be willing putty in the House-Lansing efforts to do this. All pretenses of neutrality will wane."

"In all this I cannot disagree. But why my paper?"

"Marty, I will be attacked by my many political enemies. Controlled by the wealthy corporate elite, the great newspapers will pillage me as a disloyal citizen and a "friend of the Hun." Wall Street and bankers everywhere will rejoice. No longer will I be a threat to credits and loans to London and Paris, or trade with those countries. In its infancy now the munitions' industry will grow and prosper selling instruments of death for profits in the till. They will not have to deal with my opposition. The farmers, still mired in a deep recession, will rejoice in new markets, for it will be difficult for Europe to war and plant at the same time. A harvest of profit awaits American farmers. Those who till the soil will prosper. The shipping industry will carry America's exports into the North Atlantic and into the nautical war zones proclaimed by both Great Britain and Germany. Ultimately, our shipping will be interrupted and even as merchant ships slip beneath the stormy seas companies will be awash in profits. All this I have envisioned and strenuously fought against, but to no avail."

"Still…"

"These issues might flourish for a moment as the headlines blaze with my resignation, but in time they will disappear from the front page. I will be but a blip in a few short weeks."

"Surely you will have some supporters?"

"Many, I hope. Their voices, however, will be dimmed in time and soon lost in the din of beastly headlines proclaiming the need to race headlong into a "war of choice. And that is why I have come to you, Marty."

"Exposition is necessary, please."

"You are a committed pacifist. You make no parlay with war. You, I believe, will keep the story alive and the issues dear to my heart.

You will not be deterred by political expediency or economic greed. Though the Justice Department may pounce, you will not be silenced by intimidation and threats. You, Marty, are I am afraid, a pacifist who will fight with your last breath, if not pen and ink, against the social cancer of war. Am I not right?"

A slight knocking on the door interrupted their conversation. Marty Cohen jostled from his chair and opened the door. The ubiquitous bellhop stood there, a large tray in his hands.

"Your tea and crackers, Sir."

Marty accepted the tray even as the bellhop shut the door and left.

"I ordered a little respite from the kitchen. I trust it will suffice until a more substantial lunch will be provided. But for now hot black tea and crackers with thin slices of ham and cheese."

"Very thoughtful, Marty. You will join me?"

"The crackers and cheese, yes. As to the ham …

CHAPTER 3

A SHARING OF FAITH

The two men sipped their tea and munched on their crackers, knowing full well that a little nourishment was good for the soul.

"About the ham, Marty?"

"I regret that a sour stomach and Talmudic injunctions preclude ham even in these secretive surroundings. Cheese will suffice."

"My indiscretion. I was neglectful of your Jewish background."

"It is of no concern. Still, I honor my Jewish parents. My mother was born in the Ukraine, then as now under the iron fist of the Czars and the all too familiar pogroms that dotted anti-Semitic Russia. Her side of the family migrated from Kiev to Vienna before trekking to Portugal. From there they found steerage in the bowels of a freighter headed to America. They entered the country under the watchful eyes of medical personnel at Ellis Island. From there they assimilated into the streets of New York."

"And your father?"

"The family, as fate would have it, came from a Jewish section of Budapest where they lived a tenuous life among Hungarian Christians and where again anti-Semitism often raised a tightened fist. In time the family found its way into France and from there they moved to Ireland before gaining passage to the New World and settling in New York. There my parents met. All this was before the turn of the century in the early 1880's. They kept a Kosher home and I was imbued with their dietary preferences."

"No ham?"

"No ham!"

Again quiet swept the room. It wouldn't last.

"Your family, Mr. Secretary, if I may ask? Their roots?"

"Scot, English, and Irish."

"The family well represented His Majesty's realms."

"Empires have a way of doing that."

"You are of the Christian faith?"

"Asking or declaring, Marty."

"Knowing."

"I am. My father was a Baptist. My mother was a Methodist. My parents permitted me to find my own way."

"And you did?"

"Yes. At about the age of fourteen I had a conversion experience at a religious revival. I had what some describe as an epiphany. I experienced something beyond my youthful years. In the end I accepted Jesus into my heart. It was the most important day of my life in so many ways."

"An American grown Paul of Tarsus?"

"A William Jennings Bryan in need of a loving God and a light to follow."

"And in Jesus have you found such a light."

"That and more, Marty. It carries me through the night and is the armor that serves me in battle."

"Then you are the most fortunate of men."

"You have not found such a God, Marty?"

"Regretfully, no. I am adrift. I'm afraid I have cast the Almighty aside and placed a theological bet on the human species."

"A somewhat dubious gamble, is it not?

"At times, yes, but a bet I must take."

"You don't accept the Savior?"

Marty Cohen mulled over the question or was it an accusation? Carefully he constructed his words.

"I do accept Jesus contrary to what you might think. But not the Jesus of folklore, myth, or even the Gospels; I am, I think, beyond fairy tales and a narrative tied to the supernatural. I am an unredeemed heathen who believes only in the physical man who walked in the Holy Land. In saying this, I trust I do not offend."

"A little, perhaps."

"It is my personality to do so."

"An mine to be diplomatic. So, Marty, please elaborate."

"The Jesus I know (and prefer) is the man who tried to help others, especially the weak, the poor, and the ill. The Jesus that beckons to me was devoted to a Social Gospel before the contemporary term was coined. The Jesus who challenged the moneychangers and the high priests for their wealth and position… That is the Jesus I accept. That is the Jesus who sits beside me as I write."

"But not the Gospels or the Disciples and Apostles?"

"I have no need of them, Sir. I have my own men of the cloth.

"You will share."

"If you wish. My Trinity: Sinclair, Tarbell, and Norris. My Apostles: Riis, Steffens, and Wells. My only Disciple, you."

If the walls of Room 310 of the Mason Hotel could speak, oh what they might have said:

The tall, heavy-set man stood. His jaw muscles twitched, as did his neck. His great arms were like cannon about to erupt in flame and fury. His jaw jutted out like the bow of a warship crashing though the waves. His eyes flickered and narrowed, pinpoints stabbing in the dark. For a moment the man seemed unable to speak and then slowly his great arms relaxed and his eyes registered with understanding. A knowing smile crept across his face and then a voice roared with unrestrained joy. Unable to fully control himself, the large man placed his huge arms around the smaller man and lifted him into the air like a plaything of a child before uttering only one word: "Muckraker!"

CHAPTER 4

SAINTLY WRITERS

Firmly planted back on terra firma Marty Cohen caught his breath and listened as Secretary Bryan bellowed in a voice brooking no interruption.

"Sinclair, Tarbell, and Norris indeed... All muckrakers... Journalists and writers challenging the corruption fostered by the big city political machines that siphoned off payoffs and misused taxpayer dollars... A motley group of writers disclosing the undeniable underbelly of poverty and despair in our great cities while attacking the blatant hypocrisy of the affluent and rich who flaunted their conspicuous wealth... All of them, literary to a fault, writing their novels and magazine articles to draw public awareness to the sins of our time --- child labor, unbelievable urban poverty, unsafe working conditions, and corporate corruption stifling competition in an insatiable appetite for unreasonable profit bordering on profiteering at the expense of others... "

"Sir, you must calm yourself."

"How can I do that, Marty? You have ignited a fire in me. You have reminded me of another Testament, the works of your Sinclair, Tarbell, and Norris. I am acquainted with all of them. I have read their books. I was impressed by what they wrote. They raked up the muck and filth underlying our great country. If not of the traditional

Gospels, it is of little matter. They have given us a secular scripture to ponder. They have influenced me to no end. In short, I am indebted to them."

"You know of Upton Sinclair?"

"His novel *The Jungle* (1906) revealed the terrible working conditions in the meat packing industry and the unhealthy preparation of our meat and poultry by companies disregarding health standards in their lustful greed for profits. Sinclair called our attention to the need for a federal 'meat inspection act' of some sort. This will come about. The industry lobby cannot hold back forever the need for pure food and drug legislation."

"And Ida M. Tarbell?"

"Ah, the little lady who took on the Standard Oil Company with her monumental investigative reporting --- *The Rise of the Standard Oil Company* (1902). She chronicled and condemned John D. Rockefeller's ruthless business practices and the political influence he commanded. Her work led to Washington breaking up the company's unholy monopoly permitting it to dictate prices and gouge consumers in the process. In the end he could not completely escape the long arm of the Sherman Anti-Trust Act."

"Frank Norris?"

"You speak of the author of *The Octopus* (1906)?"

"I do. His novel, as you know, portrayed the evil power of the Southern Pacific Railroad in California and how the company manipulated rates to almost turn wheat farmers into indentured servants. But that is not all... This diabolic company essentially controlled the state legislature."

"The metaphor of the octopus was apt, Marty. The tentacles of the Southern Pacific reached into every avenue of public life, distorting the California agricultural economy in the drive for greater profits. No politician in Sacramento could escape the grip of this creature.

"Saintly writers, all three of them, Sir?"

"And your Apostles, Marty?"

"Another three who strove to improve the human condition. Jacob Riis' *How the Other Half Lives* (1906). He provided an unblemished description of the slums, tenement life in New York City. Lincoln Steffens' *The Shame of Our Cities* (1904) uncovered the political corruption in our cities. And lastly, the diminutive Negro lady, Ida B. Wells, who wrote *The Free Speech* (1892) in which she condemned the flagrant flaws in our justice system that allowed, if not encouraged, lynching to occur in many states. Muckrakers all... God bless them..."

"Marty, all of them disciples of John Bunyan classic, *Pilgrim's Progress* (1687), an allegory in which a man who rejected salvation by continuing 'to rake the muck.' He focused on filth rather than eternal life."

"To remove the 'muck' is our mission, is it not, Mr. Secretary?"

"From my first days in politics to this moment, yes."

"And that is why I follow you, a disciple of a moral code I have also tried to envision through my reporting. I am not without need of a hero."

"Then we are kin, are we not for you strike a similar bell?"

"Again, that is why you are my greatest disciple Sir. That is why you are also known as the 'Great Commoner.' You seek reform where evil lurks in our society. You are progressive in your outlook. You are a man of the people. You are willing to use the power of government to improve the lives of people. You stand for a minimum wage. You argue for an eight-hour workday. You seek protection for women in the workforce. You advocate for safety regulations in our shops and factories. You oppose monopolies and fight the trusts. You are for suffrage. You demand diplomacy before embracing hostilities. . And that is why I sought this interview to better understand your thoughts on the looming war."

"You have placed a lot on my tray, Marty?"

"You have the voice to shoulder their weight."

"Perhaps we already share the burden?"

"Then, as brothers, let us proceed, Marty. A war beckons but so does my immediate resignation."

"We will, but first I must share a confession."

CHAPTER 5

A CONSCIENCE IN DISTRESS

"And what is your confession, Marty?"

"As you know I am a Socialist in good standing."

"Your political persuasion proceeds you, if your reporting is an indicator of your political leanings."

"I am also a pacifist."

"That reputation is well noted."

"I am a humanist."

"I would expect nothing less of you, Marty."

"And I am, as you know, unalterably opposed to this European calamity or the possibility of America getting involved."

"There we are in obvious agreement."

"But unlike many Socialists I am not against all wars."

It was time for a moment of reflection. Both men knew it. And questions not yet asked needed to be answered.

"You're an interesting sort of Socialist, Marty. Not all wars… You will explain."

"If attacked a person has the right to defend himself. The same is true of nations. But, of course, that is not what's happening in

Europe. No one attacked anyone, yet everyone is at war. Is that not a paradox?"

"Bordering on insanity."

"Two people are assassinated in Sarajevo by a Serbian nationalist and the world goes to hell. No armies cross borders. No hordes of soldiers descend on unsuspecting populations. No declarations of war are given. Still, vast armies are at each other's throats."

"Mobilization, Marty! That was the culprit, the snake in the Garden of Eden. Once armies began to gather to prepared war plans a collective insecurity set in causing neighbor to fear neighbor. In an unholy embrace of arms the conflict began before the first shot was fired. Only that was needed was a spark and that happened in Sarajevo."

"Your points are well taken and they lead to only one conclusion. The belligerent nations are in a war of choice, one we both seek to avoid. But there is something else, too."

"Which is, Marty?"

A conflicted Marty Cohen inhaled deeply and then paced around the room before answering.

"You will mark me as an agitator for what I am about to say."

"Possibly."

"This is a war brought on by capitalists and imperialists, by the rich and powerful to further their thirst for markets and profits. It is about empires seeking to expand and control large segments of the world. It is about exploiting workers in peacetime and continuing that exploitation through use of conscription in wartime. The workers will be forced to fight other workers thereby permitting the ruling class to profit. Out of this will only come the cries of mothers and children in orphanages … So, again I ask you, why must millions die because two members of the Austrian aristocracy were killed by a bloody anarchist?"

"Including Socialists, Marty? Are they not in the trenches, too?"

"Sadly, yes. By our nature, if not our ideology, we are opposed to war but it is not enough. We are swayed by patriotic speeches, blaring newspaper headlines, and the call of chauvinistic messages wrapped up in the clarion call of empire. French Socialists will war with German Socialists. Socialists everywhere will don the uniform of their mother country and brotherly blood will be spilled.'"

"You mentioned the role of propaganda to influence views."

"And control people, William."

War is an ugly topic. There is no joy in the subject. Both men knew that and steadied themselves for what was to come.

"The 'Rape of Belgium' is a classic example of how things can get out of hand, especially when the tabloid press and the excesses of 'yellow journalism' lock their teeth into a story."

"Propaganda or not, the events did take place, Marty."

"Unfortunately, true. The German army violated the Treaty of London dating back to 1839 that had been agreed to by Prussia. That document spelled out Belgium's firm neutrality in any conflict between the German States and France."

"But?"

"Two things happened. First, German war planners understood that any invasion of France would be through the Low Countries, and in particular Belgium. The French understood this. Second, once invaded the German Government referred to the past agreement as nothing more than a "scrap of paper.""

"That the British and American press played that up."

"To the fullest: 'poor little Belgium attacked by the Hun.'"

"And then the atrocities, Marty."

"German soldiers were accused of rape, the forced deportation of Belgium citizens to Germany to be used as slave labor... The outright murder of citizens... All this was grist for sensationalizing the news and engendering sympathy for those opposed to Berlin. Stories and graphics played up children's hands being cut off, French and Canadian soldiers crucified on doors, the breasts of nurses cut off, and the distilling of human flesh for lubricants needed by the military. The veracity of these stories was seldom questioned in an effort to convert skeptics to advance the war. Emotionalism ruled the day, hysterics the morning news. From the perspective of the Britain and France this led to but one conclusion: 'Hang the Kaiser.'"

"But there were atrocities, Marty."

"On every side, but an unforgiving war press focuses on Berlin. You know that to be the case."

"I do."

"And Wilson, House, and Lansing roll with the press."

"As does our ambassador to London, Walter Hines Page. He spends more time advocating for Britain, almost as if he's London's ambassador to Washington. He wants America to enter the war against Germany."

"And he makes use of claims about German atrocities?"

"He does."

"All warring countries engaged in this, am I not right?"

"All too true, Sir."

"So where does that leave us, Marty?"

"With the numbing feeling that the masses can be persuaded to kill. Large segments of the population can be intoxicated either with fear or the fervent hope of military glory. Either way, old men send young men into battle while others savor gory profits."

"You see that happening here, Marty?"

"Yes, as do you. The gravity toward war increases daily."

"German submarine warfare invites it."

"You speak of the sinking of the *Lusitania?*"

"I do and future ships that will be torpedoed if Germany will not stop, which I do not think she will do."

"Marty, you are not influenced by the propaganda?"

"I am not immune. Given a choice between London and Berlin, I will swim with the British with a stench in my mouth."

"The lesser of two evils?"

"Yes."

"Yet?"

"I continue to hope for mediated peace. Short of that for America to stay out of the war."

"And if we do go to war, Sir?"

"I will be a critical but supportive citizen."

"Than again we are kin, Sir."

What had been said was past the two men, and yet a prologue to what would come next.

"Mr. Secretary, I have shared my cross. The scales of time now tip to you."

CHAPTER 6

GOLD AND SILVER

"Shouldn't we move on to the issue attending this meeting, namely my resignation from the Cabinet?"

"In time, yes."

"This delay, has it a purpose, Marty?"

"Of course. If I am to support your cause, we together must connect with the reader. Political statements, no matter how eloquently written, lack something once the print ink dries. Our readers must reengage with you on some emotional level. What better way than to take them back to 1896 and the great struggle in Chicago?"

"So long ago."

"Precisely. So many who have come of age since... They know little of the battle you waged."

"Not all those memories are joyous."

"That is also true of my reporting. Nevertheless, we must try to reacquaint the past with the present. That being the case we need to go back to July 7, 1896 when the Democratic National Convention convened and the currency issue predominated."

"The decisive issue was complicated. Can you truly explain it to your readers?"

"With your help, I hope so."

"Then I shall share the events of those few days."

"I arrived in Chicago, a youthful 36-years of age, and with aspirations of winning the Democratic Party nomination. Though a 'dark horse' candidate, I had hopes of taking on the incumbent, Republican William McKinley. I arrived by train and quietly found a modest hotel room totally lacking in pomp."

"There was no overwhelming favorite for the nomination?"

"Many contenders only. No one close to the 2/3rd vote needed."

"You had a strategy?"

"Too wait in the wings until my moment, biding my time."

"You knew it would come?"

"Only one issue claimed the convention and I was the leading spokesperson on one side."

"Bimetallism!"

"Yes."

"The situation was complicated, Marty. The country was divided on the issue of our monetary standard. Was it to be solely based on gold or would silver also be used for this purpose? This was important because gold backed up our currency."

"Dollars could be redeemed for gold?"

"That was the guarantee of the federal government."

"Making gold the legal tender of the country?"

"Yes. Since that was the case, the total money supply in the country was related to the amount of gold held by the Treasury. This had been true since 1873. The more gold available, the greater the money supply, but always in a stable, reliable way where paper currency held its value, fighting off both inflation and deflation, at least in theory."

"But the problem was?"

"Marty, the banks acting as creditors wanted a non-inflationary returned on their loans and no loss of purchasing power. The debtors wanted lower interest rates and more currency by which to pay off their loans though inflation might occur. This was especially true of farmers. Our party was split over this issue."

"Which brings us, Sir, to the question of the Sherman Silver Purchaser Act of 1890."

"That legislation permitted the federal government to purchase silver to support our currency. The government pledged to stand behind the silver dollars and Treasury notes issued under the act with all coinage redeemed in gold. Again, creditors opposed this; debtors took a different position."

"And this led to your moment in the sun?"

"One July 7, 1896 the pro and anti-bimetallism forces debated the issue."

"You stood on the sidelines?"

"Until it was my turn to speak, Marty."

———————

"Though I had given hundreds of speeches across wide stretches of the country, I was a bit nervous before taking the podium. I had a way with words. Many considered me the party's chief orator. Still, I felt unease. At such times I always ate something. It seemed to calm me. I ate a sandwich. As the leading advocate of silver my speech was anticipated by a majority of the delegates who stood with me on the issue. The audience quietly prepared to hear me speak."

"Your feelings at that moment?"

"The silver issue had been glossed over the first two days of the convention in order to keep Democrats together under one tent. But it was there, burning in the night, awaiting only the right words to ignite the delegates. It was my task to provide the spark in favor of silver. No academic argument would do this, at least not alone. I had to give voice to the emotional needs of the 'common man,' who seemingly was always in debt. I had to find a way to overwhelm the anti-silver forces. I had to give the other delegates a chance to make silver the key issue in the party's platform. I began my speech."

––––––––––––

The humblest citizen in all the land, when clad in the armor of a righteous cause, is stronger than all the hosts of error. I come to speak to you in defense of a cause as holy as the cause of liberty --- the cause of humanity.

"I then turned from the general audience and spoke directly to the supporters of the gold standard. It was, I believe, my moment of reckoning."

When you come before us and tell us that we are about to disturb your business interests, we reply that you have disturbed our business interests by your course.

"You then expounded and enumerated?"

"I did. I reminded them that their definition of a businessman was 'too limited in its application.' I gave them examples:

… the man who is employed for wages is a business man…

… the attorney in a small town is as much a businessman as the corporation counsel…

… the merchant at the cross-roads store is as much a businessman as the merchant in New York…

... the farmer who goes forth in the morning and toils all day ... is a businessman...

... the miner who goes down a thousand feet into the earth is a businessman....

———————

"You electrified the audience with your litany of common folk who are the backbone of this country."

"That was the case."

"As you had hoped."

"As I had hoped."

"And then you openly challenged the moneyed class."

"It was necessary."

We do not come as aggressors. Our war is not a war of conquest; we are fighting in defense of our homes, our families, and posterity. We have petitioned, and our petitions have been scorned; we have entreated, and our entreaties have been disregarded; we have begged, and they have mocked when our calamity came. We beg no longer; we entreat no more; we petition no more. We defy...

"You crossed the Rubicon?"

"I did, Marty. There was no other course."

"And then you laid down the final challenge to your party."

Upon which side will the Democratic Party fight; upon the side of the 'idle holders of idle capital' or upon the side of 'the struggling masses?' That is the question that the party must answer first...

"You attacked."

"It was not enough. I needed to pierce the devil in his lair. I had to give a final rationale for this fight."

There are two ideas of government. There are those who believe that, if you will only legislate to make the well-to-do prosperous, their prosperity will leak through on those below. The Democratic idea, however, has been that if you legislate to make the masses prosperous, their prosperity will find its way up through every class, which rests upon them. You come to us and tell us that the great cities are in favor of the gold standard; we reply that the great cities rest upon our broad and fertile prairies. Burn down your cities and leave our farms, and your cities will spring up again as if by magic; but destroy our farms and the grass will grow in the streets of every city in the country.

"And then you said those last words that ended the debate and brought to you the party's nomination."

Having behind us the producing masses of this nation and the world, supported by the commercial interests, the laboring interests, and the toilers everywhere, we will answer their demand for a gold standard by saying to them: You shall not press down upon the brow of labor this crown of thorns; you shall not crucify mankind upon a cross of gold.

––––––––––

"What happened next, William?"
"You know."
"In your words."

––––––––––

I retreated from the podium to an unearthly silence. My god, I thought, I have failed. For a few seconds it was the most painful moment in my life. I moved toward my seat as if in a dream and then... The Coliseum burst into a wild applause and then pandemonium erupted all around me. The delegates, at least those favoring silver, threw their hats into the air. Coats and handkerchiefs soon followed. Others took up their state standards and rushed to surround the Nebraska delegation, my home state. Two alert police officers rushed toward me, hoping to prevent me from being manhandled. They were unable to do this. I was lifted to the broad shoulders of supporters who carried me around the floor.

"Your moment of triumph. The *Washington Post* described the action as 'bedlam broke loose, delirium reigned supreme.' According to police reports it took about 25-minutes to restore order. Sentiment for silver now became a powerful tonic for your nomination."

"Which would await the next day, Marty."

"Fourteen candidates competed in the first ballot. I came out second. A good start for a dark horse... On the second ballot I remained in place, but the gap was closing. The third ballot drew me even closer to the top rung. The fourth ballot moved me into first place, but I had insufficient votes; I was shy of the two-thirds ballots I needed. On the fifth ballot Illinois shifted its votes and that was it. I would represent the Democratic Party."

"The pro-gold folks were not happy.

"I was denounced for my demagoguery. Some newspapers said that lunacy dictated the platform. Others reported that hysteria reigned at the convention. I was disparaged without end. The *Wall Street Journal* dismissed me as 'having had my day.' But even my enemies admitted that one speech had swayed the convention as never before. It was a compliment, I think."

"The Republicans went right after you?"

"With pitchforks. They immediately engaged in fierce fundraising, corporate money and the wealth of the wealthy. Money was used to print pamphlets and to engage speakers to deliver a message: the Republicans stood for sound money. On the money trail I could not compete. What I could do was board a train and crisscross the country speaking on behalf of silver and the need to help debtors, the farmers, the working man, and all those oppressed by a harsh economic system."

"And in the end?"

"McKinley won."

"You did well as a candidate. You received 46,7% of the popular vote. You had 176 Electoral College votes. You won a majority of the votes in 22 states, only one less than McKinley. You earned the support of 6,510,807 people. No losing candidate had ever won so many votes. And don't forget, the vigorously fought campaign brought out over 90% of all eligible voters, almost exclusively men. You tilted against windmills with conviction and courage. Little more can be asked of anyone. Perhaps one comment from an Indiana voter summed it all up:

God has sent you amongst our people to save the poor from starvation, and we know you will save us.

"That's quite a testament, Mr. Secretary, one you would eventually take into your Cabinet position."

"And to my resignation speech tomorrow."

CHAPTER 7

CONVICTION

"Shall we begin?"

"Marty, a moment, please. Earlier you ordered in tea and crackers providing momentary substance."

"Momentary?"

"We have been at this for more than two hours."

"You are in need of further nourishment?"

"You read my mind."

"And perhaps your stomach, Mr. Secretary?"

As fate would have it at the precise moment there was again a gentle knocking at the door. Marty checked his watch, rose and went to the door, which he opened with an unusual flourish. Standing there was the hotel bellhop pushing to a large wheeled tray. Flashing a smile that was unusual for his craggy face, Marty said, "At last and on time. Enter."

The tray was smoothly propelled into the room and quickly the plates on it were efficiently placed on a writing table sufficient to support this planned feast. Covers were removed from the plates, tea was served, and the bellhop drifted out of the room, cart in hand without a word.

"You are a rascal, Marty. You're guilty of culinary premeditation at my expense."

"At my paper's expense. If fed, a nourished William Jennings Bryan would be in the appropriate mood to continue this interview."

"I accede to the wisdom of your masters."

"Shall we?"

"We shall, Marty."

The larger of the two plates showed an ample selection of fried chicken, mashed potatoes and gravy, and cooked vegetables, mainly peas and carrots. Of course, there was a platter of freshly made and nicely heated corn bread. The other plate was in reality a large bowl of hot vegetable soup. A small side dish contained a layer of dark rye bread and a healthy slab of butter. On two additional plates were large triangular wedges of apple pie.

"Marty, I take it the chicken is for me?"

"Your favorites when you barnstormed around the country giving speeches and working up an appropriate political appetite."

"You know me well."

"A good reporter should know his subject."

"I sense two meanings to your sentence."

At that two men smiled and then attacked their food with relish. Marty spooned his soup and buttered his bread enjoying both with a practiced hand. With his two hands working in unison, Secretary Bryan grasped the fried chicken in a tight grip while enjoying the buttered corn bread. It was obvious that he was an experienced practitioner given the hundreds of speeches he had delivered on the campaign trail. Focused on their lunch and soon enjoying their apple pie, the two men were at peace. Of course, that could not last. There was still work to be done.

"Sir, where do you wish to begin?"

"My looming resignation is not an event understood in a vacuum or disconnected from past events. Permit me to provide some background."

"Please."

"To begin with, Marty, the death of the Archduke, Franz Ferdinand and his wife, Sophia in the province of Bosnia was only an isolated incident, and should have remained that. In response, however, the great powers, though claiming they wanted peace, took actions that led to war. That lesson is so clear to me now and one I have shared with the president. As a nation we could fall prey to the same untimely fate. That is, though proclaiming a desire for peace, we could actually end up in a war."

"Wilson listened to you?"

"He did."

"But?"

"The President follows his own mind. In my judgment his policies will still lead to war."

"Causing you to resign?"

"Yes. Like the Europeans we will march off to a short war with bands blaring our leaders speaking of duty and honor. And like the Europeans the war will defy our expectations of relatively easy conflict. The lethal advances in artillery and the mass production of machine guns will see to that. The Europeans are dying by the hundreds of thousands and we seem determined to add to the carnage."

"There no way out of this?"

"Only the strictest neutrality can save us."

"Wilson agreed?"

"Initially, yes. He knew we needed to be neutral, "since otherwise our mixed populations would wage war on each other." Recall that one-third of our population is foreign born and has memories of the home country. Though a majority of our population has some kinship with Britain by way of language, history, and culture, we still have sizable Irish and German communities in our midst. The Irish despise the England and her control of Ireland. The Germans have allegiance to other ties."

"The view of most Americans?"

"At the outset of the conflict that we have no stake in it. Let the Europeans 'stew in their own juices."

"And now?"

"Now things are more complicated. Our economy has, as already discussed, attached itself to Europe's folly. For example, on a yearly basis before the war we exported goods and services well over $900,000,000 to Europe. As a debtor nation we needed to do this to cover the "red ink." The Europeans were creditors. Exports needed to be maintained, possibly even increased."

"Was it possible to do this? Wasn't that incompatible with a policy of strict neutrality?"

"The British and German naval blockades guarantee that outcome. It is a dilemma that has forced me to leave the cabinet."

"Reconciliation is not possible?'

"Let me put it this way. In the spirit of true neutrality and impartiality, I imposed a ban on all loans by our government to the belligerents. At first this was not a problem for the Entente, but the expense of purchasing supplies to prosecute the war has turned them into debtor nations. They are out of cash after just one year of fighting. They must borrow. They need credits. They need loans and my policy negated that."

"Wilson supported your ban?"

"At first, yes."

"Now?"

"He seeks to modified it."

"He can do this?"

"It's a matter of record. President Wilson presides over the Secretary of State. It is within his constitutional power to overrule me."

"What does he want to do?"

"He draws a fine distinction between public loans to belligerent countries as opposed to private ones. Public loans using taxpayer funds would continue to be banned. No government loans would be made. Private loans, however, would be possible. Bankers could legally extend credits and loans. They have done so already to the tune of $80,000,000 so far with almost all of it going to Britain and France. Another loan totally $500,000,000 is currently in the offering. The general public can invest in these funds seeking a healthy return on their money.

"This was all legal?"

"Marty, there was and continues to be no constitutional wall, nor are such loans considered a violation of neutrality based on American and international law."

"Which leads to a paradox, does it not, Mr. Secretary? Do we want the British and French to prevail? If so, the loans are necessary. If so, we must, it seems, favor the Entente. To deny the loans would assist Germany. A German victory would make it difficult to collect payment. Under these conditions almost any action on our part must impact the outcome of the war."

"All too true, Marty. Our improving prosperity is now linked to sales to France and Britain. The only way to extract the country from this situation was unacceptable to President Wilson, the Republicans, the farmers, the bankers, the munitions industry, and the general population. We would have to give up "freedom of the seas," and the right to trade with any nation. A complete ban would throw the country back into a recession. Even I had difficulty with that."

"And then there is the question of the naval blockades, Mr. Secretary. The British surface fleet stops our ships at sea, takes them to port, and then confiscates what they consider contraband. The German submarine fleet does not have these options. It can only torpedo ships. It is unable to care for crews and passengers. The sinking of the *Lusitania* is an example of this barbaric way of fighting a war."

"Marty, it is all uncivilized behavior with only one goal in mind: starve Germany into defeat; starve out France and Britain for the same purpose. Each side kills on the battlefield and considers civilians the foe. There is now no difference whether you kill a solder on the battlefield or starve women and children in cities. Each alliance has enacted war zones. Any neutral ship in a zone finds itself in peril. Increased trade will throw our country into this unholy mix. Wilson is considering arming our merchant ships, perhaps later escorting them in through troubled waters. Escalation will slowly entrench us in the war. Only the strictest ban on loans and ships can help us maintain our neutrality."

"Is that still possible?"

"Peace evaporates each day."

"Well then shouldn't you could stay in the cabinet and be a strident voice of dissent, William?"

"My convictions do not permit me to do that. To impede President Wilson? No. To be the only contrarian, no! I respect the president too much to do that. Our aims, I believe, are similar to stay out of the conflict. Our means by which to accomplish this have diverted. We take different roads."

Little more could be said. The two men, the journalist and the diplomat had run out of words. Now only the next day awaited them. A letter of resignation would be delivered to the White House and a news story would be filed chronicling the moment and the man behind the decision. The two men stood and shook hands, each peering intently into other. The Secretary of State then took his leave, thanking the reporter for his time and wishing him well. After a few minutes Marty Cohen sat down and prepared his news scoop.

————————

The next day a courier brought a note to the White House.

July 9, 1915
Washington

My Dear Mr. President,

It is with sincere regret that I have reached the conclusion that I should return to you the commission of Secretary of State with which you honored me at the beginning of your administration.

Obedient to your sense of duty, and actuated by the highest motives, you have prepared for transmission to the German Government a note in which I can not join without violating what I deem to be an obligation to my country, and the issue involved is of such moment that to remain a member of the cabinet would be as unfair to you as it would to the cause which is dearest to my heart, namely, the prevention of war.

I, therefore, respectfully tender my resignation, to take effect when the note is sent unless you prefer an earlier hour. Alike we are desirous of reaching a peaceful solution of the problems arising out of the use of submarines against merchantmen we find ourselves differing irreconcilably as to the methods, which should be employed.

It falls to your lot to speak officially for the nation. I consider it to be none-the-less my duty to endeavor as a private citizen to promote the end, which you have in view by means, which you do not seem at liberty to use.

In severing the intimate and pleasant relations which have existed between us during the past two years permit me to acknowledge the profound satisfaction which it has given me to be associated with you in the important work which has come before the State Department and to thank you for the courtesies extended. With the heartiest good wishes for your personal welfare and for the success of your administration I am my dear Mr. President,

Very truly yours, W.J. Bryan

PART II

GEORGE WILLIAM NORRIS

DURING PRACTICALLY ALL OF MY PUBLIC LIFE I HAVE BEEN A SINCERE ADVOCATE OF AN AGREEMENT BETWEEN THE LEADING NATIONS OF THE WORLD TO SET UP ALL THE NECESSARY INTERNATIONAL MACHINERY THAT WOULD BRING ABOUT A PRACTICAL ABOLISHMENT OF WAR BETWEEN CIVILIZED NATIONS

CHAPTER 8

THE SENATOR FROM NEBRASKA

APRIL 5, 1917 – WASHINGTON

It was a typical early spring day in the nation's capital. A bright celestial ball hung in a cloudless blue sky. A light breeze floated through the city's streets, ruffling past those already awake and walking. The predicted temperature for the city was a comfortable 73 degrees. It was Thursday and those who were employed by the government were already considering the coming weekend. Others, who worked Saturday and Sunday, were not so inclined. The streets were jammed with the new fangled Model T and its copycats, even as these new mechanical marvels still competed with horse drawn wagons. The children were by now in in school and customers were already flocking to the downtown department stores, while housewives everywhere in the city made their routine visits to the local butcher and bakery. It was just a typical early morning day in a city preparing to go to war.

At First and Main a rather handsome man dressed in a tailored suit complete with a bow tie entered the Mason Hotel. The management was expecting him, this tall dignified Nebraskan with a nicely trimmed mustache. He carried no briefcase, which was unusual for him. Under his arm, however, were three newspapers literally hot off the press. He did not stand out as he walked through the lobby. He garnered few glances. Perhaps one or two people in the crowded room might have thought, "That man looks vaguely familiar." But that was all. The man could easily be taken for a salesman, perhaps a physician, but certainly not an experienced politician who had served his state in the House of Representatives from 1903-1913, and was newly elected to the United States Senate.

The man noticed that people were looking intently at newspapers and the blaring headlines that seemed to jump out at them:

THIS MEANS WAR

AMERICA WILL AID BRITAIN

LAFAYETE, WE RETURN

MEN TO SOON BE CONSCRIPTD

The man was quite aware of the headlines and what they portended. Having participated in the grueling debate in the Senate the past few days, few people were more intimate with the implication of the Senate's vote by a clear majority to support President Wilson's call to arms. Now, as he strolled across the lobby, the man listened intently to the comments of his fellow citizens.

"The Germans are in for it now."

"Unrestricted submarine warfare forced the President's hand.

"They'll need to draft men.:

"Food prices will go up."

"Wall Street will be happy."

With these thoughts in mind, the man walked over to the front desk, stopping only to gather into his large hands a stray rubber ball, stripped and red in color. With a beaming smile, he handed the ball back to a little boy, saying, "Here you go son." At the front desk the manager acknowledged him with a knowing look and then directed him to the front elevator after providing a room number. Once in the elevator, a newly hired young man operated the mechanism as if he were at the controls of a bi-plane looping through the sky. At the third floor the gentleman departed, saying, "You should take up flying." He cautiously walked down the narrow hallway before stopping at Room 310. He tapped the door three times as requested. The door opened.

"Senator Norris?"
"Mr. Marty Cohen?"

The man entered the room and, as directed by his host, sat down in a newly placed cautioned leather chair, burnished in dark brown color.

"I appreciate your agreeing to an early morning interview. You've been through a long night in the Senate."
"A very long night, Mr. Cohen."
"Please call me Marty and how should I address you, Senator?"
"Senator."
"Of course. One question before we begin."
"Yes."
"Why have you agreed to this meeting?"
"Is that what you asked Secretary Bryan two years ago?"

"It was necessary, as it is now, Sir. Now, as to why…"

"As a Nebraskan conservative and a lifetime Republican, it's not often I sit down with an avowed Socialist."

"No matter. I sit down with avowed conservatives all the time."

"And you live to tell?"

"It pays the bills."

At that both men smiled.

"Again, why have you decided to meet with the enemy?"

"In three words, Marty: William Jennings Bryan."

"Amplification is necessary."

"I read what you wrote about that good man who placed principle and conviction above political expediency."

"Resigning from President Wilson's Cabinet was not easy for him."

"You were fair in your reporting and you always treated the former Secretary of State in a dignified manner. You also kept alive the issues that led him to that fateful decision."

"Senator, you read what I wrote?"

"Every issue of your Socialist paper. It pays to know your enemy, don't you think?"

"I do."

Again, the two men smiled.

"You wish me to do the same, Senator with…"

"My speech against war last night."

"That is covered in all the papers."

"But for how long, Marty? The country is going to war. Other headlines will claim the headlines and commentaries."

"Then I will endeavor to reflect your views as I did for Bryan who had the same journalistic concerns."

"No other reason, Marty."

"Perhaps one. I agree with your sentiments. This war we're entering is an unholy affair. The headlines do not yet attest to that."

"Then let's get going, Marty. I assumed you wish to talk about my speech to the Senate in opposition of the President?"

"I do but not yet. First, my readers need to know more about you and what you stand for. It provides human interest and enlightenment and helps my readers to relate to you."

"I bow to your journalistic whims."

"And one more thing, Senator. I took the honor of ordering some brisk but exceeding hot tea and pastries. They await you on the table."

"You knew I was a 'dry.'"

"Of course. I am also but for a different reasons."

"Which is?"

"A sour stomach."

The two men laughed.

Perhaps a bit of a jokester lurked in each of them.

"Let's begin with your earliest days, Senator."

"I was born on a farm in Sandusky County. That's in Ohio. The date was July 11, 1861 and the country was about to engage in an earlier war. My mother had eleven children. I was the second son. Unfortunately, my father who was a poor dirt farmer died when I was three. My much older brother died from wounds suffered in Resaca, Georgia when he marched with General Sherman. As was necessary, I worked the family farm and hired myself out to work my neighbor's land to earn extra money. It was always hard, physical labor. Skipping over a few things, I attended Baldwin College in Ohio and then taught public school for two years. I then attended what would later be called Valparaiso University where I studied law. As I was an excellent orator I moved easily into politics. The good people of Nebraska have seen fit to keep me employed for over a decade, one campaign after another. Sufficient background, Marty."

"It will do."

"What's next on the agenda?"

"Your three greatest, but I trust temporary failures in the House."

"You probe deeply."

"I'm a reporter."

"You speak of electricity and water in particular?"

"In a manner of speaking, yes."

CHAPTER 9

CONTROLLING
THE RIVER

'During your decade in the House you argued repeatedly for a regional plan to harness the Tennessee River. That is correct, is it not?"

"Repeatedly, I did and I never carried a victorious vote."

"The issue became personal?"

"This one, yes."

"Why, Senator?"

"Marty, recall I grew up in a family scratching a survival living off the land. I never forgot that. In the Tennessee Valley, stretching through seven states, there is a mighty untamed river that inundates the land, destroying good farmland, carrying away homes and small towns at flood time, yearly washing away God's good top soil, leaving the souls who till the land destitute. I meant to change that. This thunderous Tennessee River is over 650-miles in length. Its headwaters begin near Knoxville, Tennessee. The waters then flows southwest toward Chattanooga before turning westward through the Cumberland Plateau and into northern Alabama. It eventually joins up with the Ohio River near Paducah, Kentucky."

"The twists and turns of the river are in your mind and heart?"

"In my soul, Marty. That's where the vision is. It sustains me through the endless arguments and failing votes."

"You contend a regional approach is needed to change all this, one sponsored to a degree by the federal government."

"Yes. With so many states involved there must be a directing hand. Washington can provide that."

"This sounds a bit Socialist to me, Senator."

"It does, doesn't it?"

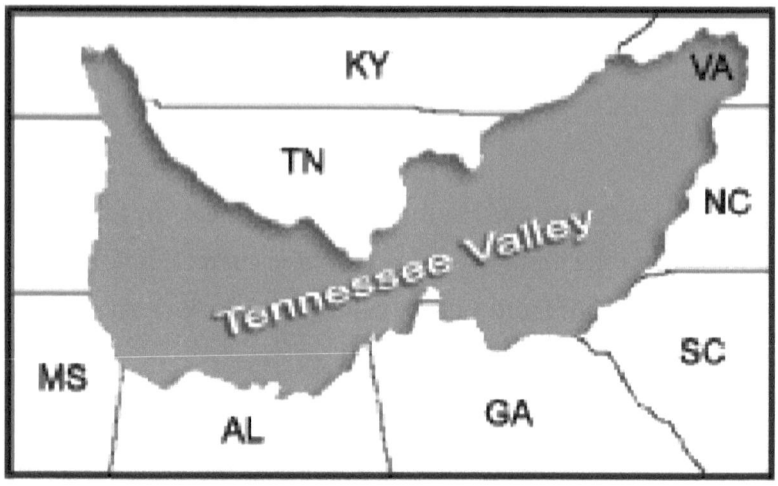

THE GREAT RIVER VALLEY

The two men gave the slightest hint of a smile. Political humor can agitate in that manner.

"You would harness the Tennessee River?"

"Yes?"

"To what ends?"

"Today the Valley is a place of economic misery. It is in dire economic straits. The average income is less than $600 per year. Over 30% of the people contract malaria. Poor family farming practices have depleted the soil, which can no longer sustain a good crop. There is no scientific rotation of the crops. Fertilizer is expensive and seldom used. The best timber has been cut and of what's left 10% is lost each year to fires."

"You paint a dismal picture."

"I see what is already on the canvas, dark and deplorable. Do you realize how many people in the Valley have no running water? How many people do not have indoor plumbing for washing, bathing, and cooking? How many people have to carry water from a stream, a lake, or a pond? And because electricity is not available too many don't have a refrigerator to store milk, butter, and eggs. Without electricity there are no electric lights to read by. There is no power for the radio to hear music or to learn the latest news. But all this can be changed. Farm income can be increased. The best farm practices can be encouraged and supported. Trees can be planted, a living resource. Navigation on the Tennessee River can be improved. An entire region can be uplifted."

"You sound like an evangelist."

"Senators wear many hats, Marty."

"And what is the key to your regional plan? What makes all this possible?"

The Senator rose, walked over to the small table, and poured himself a cupful of tea. He sipped it and then turned to his inquisitor.

"Concrete."

"Concrete?"

"Dams, Marty, at key points along the river to harness the beast. Dams will generate electricity and provide for navigable lakes. Dams, my Socialist friend. Do you know what electricity would mean for the area? Again, electricity to power lights, farm equipment, appliances used by the ladies, and power for small towns everywhere in the Valley. Industry would be encouraged to invest in the area, dependence on the land would be eased somewhat?"

"Doesn't Henry Ford want to build a private dam at Mussel Shoals?"

"That conniving 'Captain of Industry' wants to build a dam at government expense and reap the profits for his stockholders. But not while I breathe a political breath. His vision is limited to profitability. It is not regional. It is not about helping the common folk. It is a transaction for a quick buck and joy on Wall Street."

"His dam would generate electricity."

"For high, unregulated rates, Marty."

"What the market could bear?"

"That is his way."

"Still, some would benefit, is that not true?"

"Some, yes. Think bigger, Marty."

"Senator, like a Socialist?"

"Like a grinning, Socialist. I can see the great dam now, one of many. It stalks my dreams. I will see it built in my lifetime, a gracious God providing the votes."

"And your conservative friends?"

"They will unhappily weep for lost profits and investors will cry 'government intrusion in the marketplace.' I have not an ounce of pity for them."

"How would this regional development be run?"

"The federal government would own an entity, perhaps an electric utility corporation. It would receive little taxpayer funds once it was in business. It would operate like a private company and might have its headquarters in Knoxville, Tennessee. And let me add this… For the first time the government would actually know how much it costs to create electricity and to produce fertilizer. Now we only know what the industry tells us."

"It would still need to make a profit."

"A reasonable return, yes, but no more."

"Who would own this entity?"

"Much needs to be worked out, Marty, but in theory cooperatives comprised of customers (who might also be investors) would."

"Karl Marx must be smiling to hear that."

"Modern capitalism must be flexible if it is to survive. This is an opportunity for a more humane form of private sector investment."

"All this will happen, Senator?"

"It must."

"One question lingers, Sir?

"And that is?"

"How does this entity get the electricity to rural, out-of-the-way America?"

"Marty, I thought you would never ask."

"And now that I have asked?"

CHAPTER 10

STRETCHING THE LINES

"Marty, what happened when you flipped the light switch in this room?"

"The light went on."

"And if we were to turn on the radio?"

"Our ears would be assaulted by capitalist commercials."

"I won't dignify that comment though it has some merit, I must admit. If you wanted to use the telephone?"

"I would get a busy signal or a party line."

"You're being difficult."

"Because I know what you're getting at."

"And that is?"

"Millions of people living in America's rural areas lack electricity and can do none of these things. This is especially true in the Tennessee Valley that is at the heart of our discussion."

"Which brings me to another failing piece of legislation I have endlessly promoted. I have proposed that the federal government, working in partnership with private industry, electrify the entire country. The great cities have electricity. The rest of the country, particularly the most rural areas, cannot continue to be left out in the cold."

"Is that possible?"

"The private companies claim it isn't economically feasible. Their argument hinges on this. A 2300-volt system is used in our cities to distribute electricity. This relatively low voltage can be carried only about 4-miles before the voltage drops A new system is on the drawing boards. It uses a 6900-volt distribution network. This permits a much longer transmission of up to almost 40-miles. More expensive transformers would be needed along the lines and in homes, but it can be done, and at a reasonable return on investment."

What's holding it up?"

"As always, profit. The private companies won't do it."

"Why not?"

"Profits, Marty, but you knew that. They do not envision a healthy enough return on the investment."

"The federal government will have to step in?"

"Big time, Marty, beyond just money. Crews of electricians will have to travel through the countryside once the transmission lines are in place. The crews will have to add wiring to houses, barns, and offices. Ceiling mounted light fixtures would need to be installed. A single light switch would be mounted near a door everywhere. If possible, one outlet will be installed per room. You can see where this is going, Marty.

"And God said, 'Let there be light.'"

"Precisely."

"Electricians will need to be trained and some sort of cooperative, customer owned entity would have to be created. But it all can be done. All that is needed is the will to accomplish this great feat."

"And the votes, Senator."

"It will come, Marty."

"You will continue to agitate?"

"As you do, my Socialist friend. What's next, Marty? Certainly, you have a few more tricks up your journalistic sleeve before we get to last night's speech."

"I would phrase it differently, Sir, but now that you ask. Bryan had bimetallism as his rally cry. You have a unicameral mantra as part of your choir. Shall we?"

"Another one of my losing battles."

Meaning:

In a government, **unicameralism** (Latin uni, one + camera, chamber) is the practice of having one **legislative** or parliamentary chamber.

Thus, a **unicameral** parliament or **unicameral legislature** is a **legislature** which consists of one chamber or house.

Unicameral legislatures exist when there is no widely perceived need for multicameralism. Many multicameral legislatures were created to give separate voices to different sectors of society. Multiple chambers allowed for guaranteed representation of different social classes, ethnic or regional interests, or subunits of a federation. Where these factors are unimportant, in unitary states with limited regional autonomy, unicameralism often prevails.

CHAPTER 11

UNICAMERALISM

"Marty, all the states have a bicameral legislature similar to our US Congress."

"Yes, two 'houses' as they are sometimes called by political scientists."

"And often referred to as an 'upper' and 'lower' houses, such as our Senate and House of Representatives."

"With members serving for different terms, Sir. Six years in the Senate and two years in the House before standing for reelection."

"That is correct, Marty. Our Constitution spells this out, mimicking the British Parliament with its House of Lords and the House of Commons."

"A structure you are opposed to?"

"One that I have failed to change in both Nebraska and Washington D.C. regardless of my arguments."

"Still, you persist."

"I can be stubborn."

"If Nebraska adopted your plan what would the legislature look like in practice?"

"There would be from 35 to 50 members in a single house. This would provide for the greatest possible representation and a rich variety of diverse opinions."

"The term of office?"

"Possible 4-years though this is not written in concrete."

"Both political parties would be represented?"

"Of course, but those seeking office would not be listed by party affiliation."

"The majority candidate would win, I assume."

"Eventually. In the first voting round (or primary) the top two vote getters would be determined. They then would slug it out."

"Your colleagues in the House and Senate resist your overtures, Senator."

"They do and with challenging arguments. They view two chambers as a stabilizing force in keeping a majority from unduly influencing legislation, as well as lobbyists exerting too much power. They wish to spread these possibilities around as butter covers a slice of toasted bread. Many, of course, focus on the need to compromise, which, they contend is better fostered when two houses must agree to the legislation in question."

"Are there not politicians who can also use this system to delay, possibly even destroy needed legislation?"

"That can be true. But in addition, two houses requires agreement, which can also be an impediment."

"But doesn't this stabilize the political system?"

"But for whose benefit? Marty, the present system gives and takes during the innumerable process of turning a policy into law. Accountability is more difficult in a bicameral system. It is difficult at times to assign. With a sole legislative body it is easier to fix blame, depending on your views."

"Politicians cannot find your views that appealing, Sir, especially potential loss of a chamber and political positions."

"Correct. They might have to get real jobs if the store closes."

At that both men grinned. The truth is sometimes that way.

"One question, Sir. Would a single house really stop the abuse of power?"

"There are no guarantees, Marty. But I would suggest that every act would be more in the spotlight. Little could be done under the table. The simplicity of one legislative body encourages public scrutiny. And, of course, the cost to taxpayers would be reduced with only one house in session. And another point, if I may. The British system is based on having two classes of citizens, the Lords and the Commoners. Though we have a wealthy classes, we think of ourselves as a classless society. The merits of that can, of course, be debated. A unicameral system lends itself, however, to the notion of a single class of voters."

"Can what you espouse really be accomplished?"

"A vision is like a cloud, Marty. It hangs in the sky, then dissipates only to return later in some altered form, but it always returns. My determination is much the same.

A slight tapping of the door interrupted their now whimsical discussion of parliamentary venues. Marty excused himself and then strolled to the door, already knowing what lurked behind it. A bellhop stood there saying nary a word. Then, as if in a choreographed play, he entered the room, pushing along the ubiquitous wheeled-food cart. Sill silent as the midnight hours he placed dishes on a table, along with utensils and cloth napkins. It took but a moment and then he was gone, already aware of the generous gratuity that awaited him at the front desk.

"What's this, Marty."

"I took the liberty of ordering a bit of sustenance. Chicken salads and bread fresh from the oven."

"Something easy for our stomachs?"

"And our political views."

"And after dining you'll finally turn to my speech?"

Marty Cohen didn't answer immediately. Rather, he served up healthy portions for each before saying, "A short but necessary aside. We must go to sea with names with which you are familiar --- The Thrasher Incident and the *SS Arabic*."

"You have done considerable research."

"My readers need to know your views."

"Then to my speech?"

"Yes."

"This is journalistic extortion."

"True but for a good cause."

CHAPTER 12

THE THRASHER INCIDENT

"Senator, you recall the name Leon Chester Thrasher?"

"In a melancholy manner, yes."

"His body was washed ashore on Ireland's coast on July 11, 1915 after it had been in the water 106 days according to the authorities."

"And he was an American citizen?"

"A mining engineer from Massachusetts."

"And?"

"He had been aboard the *SS Falaba*, a British steamship that left Liverpool for West Africa. She was torpedoed by the *U-28*, one of 30 German submarines operating in and around British Isles as part of Berlin's naval blockade. One hundred and four people died, crew and passengers out of a total of 242 souls aboard the steamship."

"And Leon Chester Thrasher?"

"The lone American aboard the ship and the first American citizen to die in the European conflict due to the war at sea."

"A dubious honor for the poor man."

THRASHER

"The circumstances surrounding the events of March 28, 1915…
You recall them, Sir?"

"They are emblazoned in my memory. Captain Frcdcrick Davies
of the *Falaba* was ordered to stop and abandon the ship before it was
sunk. He did so but took excessive time in evacuating the vessel.
Apparently it was a very disorganized efforts. Confusion, it seems,
reigned. But there is another aspect to this. Later testimony indicated
that the slow evacuation was partly due to the Captain Davis' efforts
to radio the position of the *U-28* to a nearby British patrol ship,
which quickly responded to his signal. Unable to wait --- and before
all passengers and crew were fully off-loaded --- the submarine
fired a single lethal torpedo.. Over thirteen tons of highly explosive
contraband ignited and the ship quickly sank."

"The press played up the sinking?"

"On both sides of the Atlantic, Marty."

"You were newly elected to the Senate?"

"A Nebraskan who was impressed by the on-going response of President Wilson and Secretary Bryan to the blockade business. Only a few months before the sinking, they had called the German blockade 'an act so unprecedented in naval warfare' that Berlin would be held to 'strict accountability for such acts.' That position strongly suggested the United States would take 'any necessary act in sustaining the rights of its citizens or in safeguarding the sacred duties of international law."

"You agreed with these positions?"

"In large measure, yes. A response was necessary."

"Without reservation?"

"Not completely. I was already wondering what was at the end of this road?"

"Meaning, Senator?"

"Carried to its logical conclusion was war an outcome of these first piecemeal measures? This was on my mind, along with one other thing."

"Which was?"

"The submarine, though sinister and deadly when lurking beneath the waves, is fragile and vulnerable when it surfaces. By its very nature it must attack and then disappear into the depths. A submarine does not have the time or the physical space to make provisions for the safety of passengers. That being the case there will be more 'incidents' if 'unrestricted warfare' continues. Having no choice, the Wilson Administration will be forced to respond with increasingly bold language."

"Senator, is not freedom of the seas' at stake here, as well as the rights of Americans to travel or trade?"

"As is our effort to remain neutral in this war. I don't think we can have both, strict neutrality and traditional freedoms at sea. Something must give."

"You knew of the Gore-McLemore Resolution?"

"Yes and I would have supported it."

"Is it your understanding that the resolution would require the President to warn Americans against traveling aboard foreign ships 'of belligerent nations' to avoid another Thrasher Incident?"

"That and, if necessary, confiscating the passports of citizens who failed to comply."

"It didn't pass Congress."

"The public supported it?"

"The public, as is often the case, was divided on the issue."

Marty Cohen knew it was time to move on. Another ship awaited the two men.

"Let's turn to the events surrounding the SS *Arabic*."

CHAPTER 13

ANOTHER INCIDENT

"You also know of the sinking of the *SS Arabic*?"

"I do, Marty."

"August 19, 1915... A sad day off the coast of Ireland... Another submarine attack by a German submarine..."

"The *SS Arabic* was a British registered passenger ship owned by the White Star Line. She was dispatched to her untimely fate by the *U-24*. Forty-four passengers and crew died, including three Americans. Our fellow countrymen were enraged by the headlines."

"The ship was outward bound for the United States. Once torpedoed she sank within ten minutes. The sinking appeared to be deliberate. The *U-24* made no provisions were made for safety of the crew and passengers."

"Wilson's hands were again being forced, Senator."

"As were the Kaiser's paws."

"The United States could protest and publicly act strong, but the truth was the country was totally unprepared for war, even if the public was fully supportive of that course, and it wasn't."

"The Germans too were conflicted, Sir. If they continued "unrestricted naval warfare,' the US might be pushed into the war, unprepared or not. But to stop the naval strategy was also dangerous.

This would permit the British continue their surface blockade while making it difficult for Germany to starve London into submission."

SS ARABIC

"Berlin found a mid-position, Marty. New orders were issued to the U-boat commanders. Until further notice, all passenger ships would only be sunk after being warned. Time would be permitted for evacuate the passengers and crew. This 'compromise' was acceptable to President Wilson and the new Secretary of State, Robert Lansing."

"Acceptable until, of course, the next incident."

"Policy is always constrained by reality. A misjudgment by a U-boat commander... A cruise ship threatening to ram a submarine..."

"You are not optimistic?"

"Marty, war is like gravity. It exerts a continuous pull. Nothing can escape it."

"Still, you resist this universal law?"

"A law made by men, not, I suspect, a natural law."

"In the end?"

"War will overwhelm us."

"If I may ask, where is God in all this?"

"As a good Socialist, pacifist, and agonistic, you tell me, Marty."

"You know of my Jewish background?"

"I am not unaware of your views. That being the case, how do you answer my question?

"God, I think, is sitting this one out. After all, which of his children should he save, the French Catholic or the German Protestant? Which child should he protect, the boy in Austria or the girl in Belgium? Which home should burn to the ground, a peasant hovel in Russia, or a mansion in Vienna? I pity God for having to deal with all this. I wouldn't blame the Supreme Being for taking leave of all of this."

"It's our mess?"

"Can there be any other explanation?"

As it must be it was time to move on to the Senator's speech.

CHAPTER 14

THE DAY BEFORE

APRIL 4, 1917

"Senator, your speech was long, listing as you did in great detail, the events leading up to your opposition to President Wilson. With that in mind I need you list and explain your main points. That will assist me and in time my readers. I trust that is agreeable?"

"Of course. I wouldn't want your Socialist readership to have doubts as to my position."

"And, as we progress, you will permit me to act as a devil's advocate?"

"With as little fire and brimstone as possible, yes."

"Then, Sir, begin as you will."

––––––––––––

"As I stood to speak I realized I was in a distinct but honorable minority. President Wilson wanted to arm American merchant ships and the Senate concurred. The same was true for the House. This was the reality of the situation. Eloquence alone would avail little. Flowing oratory was not enough. Minds had already been made up. This I realized. Therefore, what tact should I take? I decided to simply and quietly lay out the series of events that had brought the country to this point. If I could not change votes, I could at least explain to my Nebraska voters where I stood.

"I began by saying the obvious:

I am most emphatically and sincerely opposed to taking any step that will force our country in the useless and senseless war now being waged in Europe.

The resolution before the Senate is a declaration of war. Before taking this momentous step...we ought to pause and calmly and judiciously consider the terrible consequences of the step we are about to take.

The reason given by the President in asking Congress to declare war against Germany is that the German Government has declared certain war zones in which, by the use of submarines, she sinks, without notice, American ships and destroys American lives...

———————

"You then pointed out, I believe, that the first war zone was declared by Great Britain, November 4, 1914. The Germans made their declaration in response in February 1915. You then challenged both London and Berlin."

"I did and in strong language."

It is sufficient to say that our government has officially declared both of them (war zones) to be illegal and has officially protested against both of them. The only difference is that in the case of Germany we have persisted in our protest, while the case of England we have submitted.

———————

"We were showing, were we not Senator, a distinct pro-Britain favoritism."

"Neutrality favoring the British, yes."

"But we could have defied both blockades?"

"Yes, Marty, and risked war."

"We could have also acquiesced in both cases, bowing to Britain and Germany."

"And remained neutral… But that would have required a powerful message to vested interests, which I stated in my speech.

> *We could have said … while these orders (war zones) are both contrary to international law and are both unjust, we do not believe that the provocation is sufficient to cause us to go to war for the defense of our rights as a neutral nation, and, therefore, American ships and American citizens will go into these zones at their own peril and risk.*

———————————

"American pride and more made it difficult to take that tact."

"As you say, Marty. But other forces were also at work to deny the strictest neutrality. The public has been misled as to the real history and true facts by great wealth that has a 'direct financial interest in our preparation in the war.'"

"You then challenged that wealth."

> *It is now demanded that the American citizens shall be used as insurance policies to guarantee the safe delivery of munitions of war to belligerent nations. The enormous profits of manufacturers, stockbrokers, and bond dealers (has) further increased by our entrance into the war. This has brought us to the present moment …*

We have loaned many hundreds of millions of dollars to the Allies (Britain and France) in this controversy. While such actions were legal and countenanced by international law, there is no doubt in my mind but the enormous amount of money loaned to the Allies in this country has been instrumental in bringing about a public sentiment in favor of our country taking a course that would make every bond worth a hundred cents on the dollar and making the payment of every debt certain and sure.

———————————

"You then challenged entrenched economic interests by turning their own words upon them."

"Marty, I did because it was necessary, but I did so with a heavy heart."

"You spoke the truth."

"As I had the light to understand it."

"You quoted directly from a letter written by a member of the New York Stock Exchange."

———————————

Regarding the war as inevitable, Wall Street believes that it would be preferable to this uncertainty about the actual date of its commencement. The popular view is that stocks would have a quick, clear, and sharp reaction immediately upon outbreak of hostilities, and that they then would enjoy an old-fashioned bull market such as followed the outbreak of war with Spain in 1898. If the United States does not go to war, it is nevertheless good opinion that the preparedness program will compensate in good measure for the loss of the stimulus of actual war.

"After providing this citation you said, 'Here we have the cold-blooded proposition that war brings prosperity to that class of people who will benefit from hostilities."

"I did."

"And then you asked a single-minded question, did you not? Who wouldn't benefit from war?"

"Not the soldier who will fight for $16 per month as he sheds his blood. Not the broken-hearted widow 'who awaits the return of the mangled body of her husband.' Not the mother who 'weeps at the death of her brave boy.' Not to the little children who shiver with cold… War brings no prosperity to the great mass of common and patriotic citizens. War only brings prosperity to the stock gambler on Wall Street who are 'already in possession of more wealth than can be realized or enjoyed.'"

"Your words were powerful."

"But not sufficient, Marty.

"But you did warn your colleagues."

> We are taking a step that is fraught with untold danger. We are going into war upon the command of gold. We are about to do the bidding of wealth's terrible mandate. By our act we will make millions of our countrymen suffer… all because we want to preserve the commercial right of American citizens to deliver munitions of war to belligerent nations.

————————————

The Senator stopped speaking. He could say no more.

"Senator Norris, you are kin with William Jennings Bryan."

"And perhaps the two of us, grizzled old politicians, are also kin with a certain Socialist reporter."

At that the two men smiled. They then stood and shook hands before departing the Mason Hotel. It had been a long day and a longer night loomed.

PART III

JEANNETTE RANKIN

THERE CAN BE NO COMPROMISE WITH WAR. IT CANNOT BE REFORMED OR CONTROLLED, CANNOT BE DISCIPLINED INTO DECENCY OR CODIFIED INTO COMMON SENSE. FOR WAR IS THE SLAUGHTER OF HUMAN BEINGS TEMPORARILY REGARDED AS ENEMIES ON AS LARGE A SCALE AS POSSIBLE.

CHAPTER 15

THE LADY FROM MONTANA

LUNCH WITH A RADICAL – JULY 1917

The lobby of the Mason Hotel was jam-packed with guests, most of whom were new to Washington. Unable to get reservations in more fashionable locations or being held on a tight rein by their employers, the old hotel seemed like a good bet. It was only a quick walk from First and Main Streets to the Congress Building, the many federal offices, and, if one was inspired, not too far from a peek at the White House. For the many men in the lobby, most of whom were contractor or agents for companies bidding for war contracts, the Mason was convenient for their purposes. Almost to a man they smoked Cuban cigars, puffing and huffing their way through the hotel, leaving behind them a cloud of Caribbean haze, what some might deem "revenge of the Spanish." Seemingly, they all wore three-piece suits, obviously off the rack and buttoned from belt to neck. If one looked closely, each man had a wad of little white cards that he dispensed with practiced ease to other men who, of course, reciprocated.

Things were buzzing. There was no question about that. The hotel management had anticipated the action.. Every room was full, lots of booze was ordered, somewhat salacious parties seemed without end, the hotel's eating room was in constant demand, and healthy tips flowed day and night. Prosperity was no longer just around the block. After all, three months ago the country had cheerfully embarked on "Mr. Wilson's War" to make the world safe for democracy and the war economy' was taking off.

Of course, there were many women in the lobby. Some were wives, others were lady friends, a few were professionals with notebooks, plus the young and old who cleaned, served, and kept the hotel running. Where the ladies did congregate there was a sea of expansive hats, many with flowers and feathers, and bright, colorful ribbons adorning them. The ladies, one speculated, chatted about the latest fashions and the explosion of social activity in the city. A keen listener might have heard, however, a few comments about the most famous woman in town and it wasn't the president's wife.

"What do you think of her?"
"Her dress or her vote?"

"She seems able to deal with the men, don't you think?"
"It remains to be seen how they deal with her?"

"She's for suffrage, right?"
"The unrestricted universal vote, yes."

"She's taking a lot of heat for saying 'no' to the President, isn't that so?

"She put her career on the line the same day she was sworn into office. Can you believe that?

Lost in their conversation these ladies missed seeing the object of their discussion. Into the lobby walked a woman wearing a wide-brimmed white straw hat with very thin red, white, and blue ribbons fashioned to it. Her simple dress was blue in color. A light jacket added to an attractive profile. She carried a large purse, slung over one shoulder. A cursory look into the purse would have found two daily papers, dated July 6, 1917, and a raft of documents related to her work. She moved with a purposeful gait to the front desk, where the management acknowledged her with a barely discernable nod and whispered prepared words: "He's in the back of the dining room, last table on the far right, somewhat secluded from most of the folks."

The woman, slim and trim, and bronzed by the Montana sun, thanked the desk clerk and quickly walked into the dining room that was now catering to the lunch crowd. It took her a moment to find the table in question. She approached the table with a mixture of anticipation and curiosity, wondering which emotion would most color her day. As she approached a nicely dressed man rose, extended his hand, before saying:

"Miss Jeannette Rankin?"

"Mr. Marty Cohen?"

CHAPTER 16

SIZING EACH OTHER UP

"I have been told you met Senator Norris in a hotel room, not in a busy, very crowded dining room."

"You were informed correctly."

"That was also true of your meeting with Secretary of State Bryan?"

"It was."

"But in my case?"

"Decorum."

"I am an emancipated woman."

"One now with political enemies, and I'm a married man. We must keep up appearances. Meeting in a hotel room would not, I suggest, benefit either one of us. Those who are critics would make baseless charges. That is why we meet here."

"But with so many people?"

"Our best cover. We will be lost in the din. Anyway, who would expect the first American woman in Congress to dine at the Hotel Mason with a hard-nosed reporter with a Socialist newspaper?"

"And the only woman in Congress."

"That, I think, is only a temporary state of affairs, Miss Rankin."

"You're for suffrage?"

"I'm for many things."

"I was told to be on my guard with you."

"Good advice."

"That you're a bulldog for a story."

"Alas, true."

"But that you are fair and honest with your reporting."

"Within limits, yes."

Though Senator Norris had spoken to her about Marty Cohen, she still wasn't sure what she was getting into. The slight man across from her had requested an interview from her first day in Washington. She had put him off. He was persistent. She harbored concerns. She was unsure about giving an interview to an unapologetic Socialist. But he had sent her his articles on the Senator, which she read and appreciated. He had written a balanced report of the Senator's opposition to the war. Whatever his personal views, he had been as objective as possible or so she thought. And that was what she wanted.

"Miss Rankin, I have ordered Irish stew, a salad, and coffee. I trust that meets your approval?"

"It does, Mr. Cohen."

"Marty, please."

"And before you ask, Marty, Jean will be fine."

"Jean?"

"My alias for our meeting. It's the adventurist in me. A mysterious meeting with a enigmatic name."

"Well, then it's Jean as you wish. Why did you finally agree to meet with me?"

"My answer will not surprise you. As in the cases of Secretary Bryan and Senator Norris, I want my views to outlast the temporary journalist madness perpetuated by the tabloid press and others, and the frenzy of accusations and repudiations my vote has inspired. This you did for them and, I hope, for me."

"I will do what is possible."

"Where do we begin? With my vote?"

"Oh, no. First we dine and then we slip into the past, covering a few things before turning to April 6, 1917."

"That will help?"

"The reader must know who you are beyond your vote."

"You will probe?"

"It is what I do, dear lady."

CHAPTER 17

OUT WEST

"Before we begin, Marty."

"Yes?"

"No questions about my personal life. Okay?"

"As you wish."

"Nor my relationship with my brother."

"Wellington?"

"Yes."

"Certainly."

"Then, begin."

You were born in Montana?"

"On the Grant Creek Ranch nine years before the Montana Territory became a state. That was on July 7, 1880."

"On a ranch?"

"Near Missoula."

"It always helps to have a point of reference."

"I agree."

"Your parents, Jean?"

"My mother was a teacher. She came from New England. My father was a mill owner. He was born in Canada."

"You came from a large family?"

"I was the oldest of six children, five girls and one boy, Wellington. He was the youthful king of our roost."

"And perhaps some of the magic behind your election victory?"

"You know of him?"

"He financed your House campaign and also directed it."

"You did your research."

"I read a few Montana newspapers. He occupies a prominent place within the state's Republican Party."

"Nothing else, Marty?"

"Jean, he counseled against opposing President Wilson."

"He was being pragmatic."

"And"

"I had to stand by my convictions."

If possible, the lunch crowd seemed to have grown in size and sound. Every table was packed, so much so that additional chairs had been brought in for the hungry guests. Secluded in their corner of the room at a table for two, Marty Cohen and Jeannette Rankin were secure from prying ears. Except for an occasional jostling by guests on the move, they were essentially, as Marty hoped, camouflaged in their little corner of the world. The clatter of dishes and the high-spirited voices gave additional cover to their meeting.

"Life was hard on the ranch, Jean?"

"Farming and ranching required long hours and physical labor. My sisters and I worked along side the ranch hands. I seemed adept at construction work and maintaining equipment."

"Equality on the frontier."

"With labor, yes, but not with the vote. I picked up on that from my mother. Women didn't have a equal political voice."

"An on-going issue for you?"

"As you say, on-going."

"Perhaps we could move on. You graduated from the University of Montana in 1898 just in time for T.R.'s frolics in the Spanish-American War."

"I earned a degree in biology."

"Then?"

"I tried teaching, dressmaking, and designing furniture. Eventually, I moved to San Francisco where I worked in the Telegraph Hill Settlement House. There I became interested in social work. This seemed to be my calling. For the first time I became intensely involved with immigrants and their children. I learned about the working conditions in factories, and wage legislation that kept people poor. I learned about labor laws. It was a whole new world opening up to me."

"Which you decided to pursue?"

"I enrolled in a graduate program the New York School for Philanthropy in New York City. Today the school is known as Columbia University. All that was in 1898-1899."

"Sociology was a new field?"

"Yes. While in New York I worked in police courts at night, attempting to assist workers who had been exploited. It was not easy work, but it was eye-opening."

"It was at this time that you became involved with the Heterodoxy Club in Greenwich Village?

"Marty, you have been at work."

"This topic came up as I was researching for our interview."

"And, if I may ask, what did you learn?

"You were part of a women's club of activists and reformers. Many of the women were suffragists, peace activists, artists, and journalists."

"Others, Marty, were authors, scientists, lawyers, actresses, and playwrights."

"Under the banner of Heterodoxy, which, as I understand it, means 'unorthodox.'"

"It does. It was a place where women could meet. The Club provided a forum to debate the issues of the day, especially those bearing on women. The group met on alternate Saturdays at Polly's Café on MacDougal Street in New York. It was founded in 1912 by Marie Jenney Howe. There was only one requirement for membership. The applicant could 'not be orthodox in her opinion.' Diverse political views were encouraged."

"Which you found fascinating?"

"Intoxicating."

"You were influenced by your involvement?"

"How could I not be. Some of our guest speakers included Helen Keller and Margaret Sanger. They had much to say and I listened."

"Nothing else, Jean?"

"As a well-educated woman it was a pleasure to associate with other such women. As an outspoken woman pushing against the social restraints of the time, it was important to know I was not alone.

"You became a professional Social Worker?"

"I did. I moved to Spokane, Washington where I worked with children in need through the Washington Children's Home Society. I found foster homes for abandoned children. It was difficult but rewarding work."

"There were many children?"

"Far too many."

"You then moved on to the University of Washington for further studies."

"I did. I took courses in economics, political science and history. It was there that I got involved in the women's suffrage movement."

"That fostered a new chapter in your life?"

"Like a duck to water, as they say, I quickly entrenched myself in the crusade. I had found a world in which I could be effective. I gave many speeches. In time I grew as a suffrage advocate. I, it seemed, had a talent for passionate public speaking. In some quarters I became known for my speeches on street corners, at fairs, at farmers' meetings, as well as in churches."

"Your work paid off."

"Yes. In November 1910 Washington became the fifth state to permanently franchise women. The continuing battle in other states called to me."

DEMONSTRATING FOR THE VOTE

"I returned to New York. There I helped organize the New York Woman Suffrage Party. Our goal was to promote suffrage in the State Legislature. It was there I became involved with NAWSA."

"With?"

"The National Women's Suffrage Association."

"Jean, I have only slight knowledge of this organization. Perhaps you would fill in the gaps."

"NAWSA was formed on May 15, 1869. Its two most famous leaders were Susan B. Anthony and Elizabeth Cady Stanton. The primary function of the group was to extend to women the right to vote. The basic argument was that the Constitution implicitly enfranchised women by its guarantees of equal protection under the laws and for all citizens."

"You became a lobbyist for NAWSA?"

"I did. I traveled to Washington to lobby Congress."

"You were successful?"

"Initially, no, but I did gain valuable experience, which helped me when I returned to Montana to become President of the Montana Women's Suffrage Association. I became, Marty, the first woman to address the Montana legislature, arguing on behalf of suffrage. That was on February 1, 1910. After my speech I was presented with small bouquet of violets. The flowers were nice, but what I really wanted were votes to pass the needed legislation."

"You were not successful this time?"

"Correct. But I had faith that ultimately the legislation would prevail and it did. In November 1914 Montana became the seventh state to grant universal unrestricted suffrage."

"You spoke eloquently on the topic at that time."

All over the country women are asking for the vote... We are a force in life, a factor, which must be considered in all problems... While we Montana women have broader opportunities than the women of any other part of the world, we want the ballot in order to give opportunity to less fortunate women. The Census Reports show what there are eight million women engaged in manual labor in this country. They are not there because they don't want to stay at home, but because hey must work if they are to live.

"About this time you also became the national field secretary of NAWSA."

"Yes. It was my job to travel the country, providing support to state suffrage organizations. I did so in fifteen states, including Ohio, Delaware, Florida, and California. This proved an invaluable experience in preparing me for the next stage in my life."

"Running for political office?"

"Joining the boys, Marty."

CHAPTER 18

RUNNING

"Sometime in early 1916 I made the decision to run for Congress."

"You had been thinking about this for some time?'

"As they say, on and off."

"Why?"

"Marty, I was tired of lobbying those in power. If elected, I could promote suffrage from inside the halls of power."

"You spoke to your brother?"

"Wellington was in favor with three conditions."

"Which were, Jean?"

"First, he would finance the campaign. As a successful attorney he had the cash. Second, he would serve as my campaign manager. Someone had to be in charge. He had political experience. I didn't. Third, he would provide political advice. As a Republican with deep roots in the state, he had his finger on the pulse of Montana's folks. I accepted all three conditions. However, I did point out the obvious. I was a person of strong convictions."

"You would be discerning in following his advice?"

"And independent."

"He knew that?"

"Oh, yes."

"An opportunity to run came about?"

"In 1916 there were two at-large House seats up for grabs. The state did not yet have Congressional Districts. The election would be statewide."

"Did you know what you were getting into?"

"Hardly, but I quickly learned. Given Montana's sparse population spread across an immense piece of real estate, the need to campaign beyond the few urban centers was the first challenge. To win I would have to reach out to remote ranches and farms, small towns off the beaten path, and into hamlets where only the railroad connected these folks to the outside world."

"Your decision to run was seen by many as audacious, was it not?"

"Certainly. While suffragists wanted a woman in political office, but running for Congress was considered something perhaps a bit too lofty. I was urged to run for a local office."

"You were not deterred?

"I was determined."

"By the way you campaigned that became obvious. Jean, you campaigned, as I understand it, everywhere, day and night."

"I traveled widely by train to reach our scattered population. I met people in schoolhouses, on street corners, at their ranches, on their farms. I got used to rubber chicken for meals and potluck suppers under the starry skies of Montana. In the cities I walked the pavement, almost house-to-house in my quest for votes."

"What were your main issues?"

"Suffrage, as you can imagine was a primary focus. Assistance, where needed, for ranchers and farmers was important. I supported prohibition though many of my fellow citizens enjoyed hard liquor. As a pacifist, I ran as a peace candidate. I made no secret of that."

"And as a social worker?"

"Whatever could be done to help the family I supported."

"Labor?"

"I favored the right of workers to organize."

"You had progressive agenda."

"If you say so."

"You were successful in the primary?"

"Including myself there were eight Republicans in the race. I received the most votes. I would be in the general election in November, where the top two vote getters were assured of office."

"The opposition mounted a spirited opposition?"

"Led by the largest employer in Montana, yes."

"The Anaconda Copper Company?"

"That also owned or controlled most of the newspapers in Montana. At first the opposition tried to merely ignore my candidacy, a sort of fluke, a sideshow with little merit. As the campaign picked up so did the efforts to disparage a woman running for Congress. Lastly, my policies were attacked, especially my pacifist leanings."

"Still, you won."

"Yes, by coming in second, I did. The voters elected me to go to Washington."

"The vote of women helped?"

"Immensely. I knew the women of Montana 'would stay by me.' The 'women worked splendidly, and I am sure they felt that the results have been worth the effort.'"

"How did you feel election night?"

"As the results settled in I was 'deeply conscious of the responsibility resting upon me.' I knew it was wonderful 'to have the opportunity to be the first woman to sit in Congress.' At the same time the seriousness of the situation weighed on me. I knew I would not only 'represent the women of Montana, but also the women of the country.' I knew I had my work 'cut out for me.'"

"You became an instant celebrity?"

"Marty, the press descended on Montana. Almost overnight I found myself under a microscope. The press made comments about the color of my hair, the clothes I wore, and the recipes I used. I was asked to promote commercial products for an insane amount of money. Offers of marriage besieged me, as did offers to join speaking tours."

"Sounds like a circus?"

"That was just the beginning. I knew I was being held to impossible standards and expectations beginning with how I would deal with men. Would I giggle? Would I act silly before masculine beards and mustaches? Would I be too hail-fellow? Obviously, the press didn't know me. I was used to dealing with rough men on the ranch. I was self-possessed. I was a sensible woman who had campaigned for suffrage and for elective office. I was a serious person with a job to do in Washington."

"Which began on April 2, 1917?"

"The most fateful day in my life."

CHAPTER 19

IMPULSES

"Before we move on, Jean…"

"Yes?"

"I assume there were any number of influences in your life. Was one of them the notion of a Social Gospel?"

"I am aware of the theology behind the concept, namely that no Second Coming was possible until 'humankind rid itself of social evils by human effort.' It was a sort of post-millennial Christian view of what could be, a biblical injunction for improving the secular world. Most appropriately it's based on the Lord's Prayer, Matthew 6:10: '… your kingdom come, you will be done, on earth as it is in heaven.' The Social Gospel represented hope voiced by Christian ministers who wanted to put into practice a Christian ethic to provide for social justice."

"That meant?"

"Struggling against poverty, economic inequality, crime, alcoholism, the worst of the slums, and to improve schools for all children. In 1879 the goals of a Social Gospel were outlined as such:

The great ends of the church are the proclamation of the Gospel
for the solution of humankind; shelters, nurture, and spiritual
fellowship of the Children of God; the maintenance of divine

worship; the prosecution of truth; the promotion of social righteousness; and the exhibition of the Kingdom of Heaven in the world.

"Fine words and, if I may add, very Jewish."

"I am told you are of that persuasion."

"It seems kin to my Socialistic leanings."

"Then perhaps a little of the Old Testament has seeped into my Protestant upbringing."

"Perhaps. Now, as to the Social Gospel."

"It was a religious justification and rationale for a call to action to alleviate social problems."

"In practice?"

"It meant moving past the 'selfishness of the individual' to the 'selfishness of institutions."

"Meaning exactly what?"

"The Social Order must change to provide social justice.

"Jean, now you sound very much like a Socialist."

"You won't tell anyone?"

"Your secret is safe with me."

Marty Cohen knew it was time to pause and to consider the implication of what had been said. Jeannette Rankin knew this, too. They each knew what would come next.

"Jean, how would this work on a practical basis?"

"I give you as a child of the Progressive Era and a disciple of the Social Gospel, Thomas Uzzel. He preached in the Methodist People's Tabernacle in Denver, Colorado. He established communal services for his congregation and others in need. What did that include?

- a free dispensary
- services for medical emergencies
- an unemployment bureau for job seekers
- a summer camp for children
- a night school for extended learning
- a kindergarten
- a food bank to provide food and milk for children
- English learning classes for immigrants

"He sounds like a man ahead of his times."

"He was. Federal and state programs were little and in many cases ineffectual. Where other charities provided limit assistance, he tried to cover the bases, A to Z. As the sociologist would say, he approached social problems in a holistic manner."

"If you had to sum up his efforts, Jean?

"To protect the children. To protect the family."

"Nothing more?"

"To end the sin of child labor."

BOYS IN THE COAL MINES

"Does that clarify things, Marty?"

"To end the evils of capitalism!"

"Not the system, only its evils."

"You brought these views to Washington?"

"I did."

"And they led to your involvement with what would eventually be called the Sheppard-Towner Act?"

"Yes."

"Tell me about that."

———————————

"I was acquainted with the views of Senator Morris Sheppard of Texas and Representative Horace Mann Towner of Iowa when I arrived in Washington. They were piecing together legislation to assist pregnant woman and to ensure the safe delivery of babies. There was a real need for such services. Over 80% of all expectant mothers did not receive any advice or trained care. There was an exceptionally high rate of infant and maternal mortality in the United States. The infant mortality rate was 111.2 deaths per 1000 births, the highest of any industrialized country. The problem was especially acute in rural areas where women had limited access to professional medical treatment. And, as might be expected, there was a high correlation between poverty and the mortality rate."

"In practice what would be done?"

"The hopeful legislation would provide hygiene instruction, including infancy child care. Public nurses would do this. Visiting nurses would be part of the program. Consultation centers would be established. Printed educational materials would be provided. The regulation and licensing of midwives would be instituted. The federal government would issue funds to the states on a dollar for dollar basis. It would be a partnership of matching funds."

————————

You would work for that legislation?"

"I had every intention to do so."

"But?"

"I ran into a sledgehammer called history."

"President Wilson?"

CHAPTER 20

THE RESOLUTION

APRIL 2, 1917

"Jean, you were sworn in by Champ Clark, the Speaker of the House from Missouri, on April 2, 1917?"

"I was. It was a Monday, a lovely day."

"One you had looked forward to?"

"With bated breath, as they say."

"The news reports stated the Congress stood and gave you sustained applause."

"It was my special moment, and for all women. The accolades were genuine and appreciated. But since I was now the only American woman in the United States Congress, I must admit, I did felt terribly alone. I had to struggle against that feelings. I kept reminding myself that other women would follow. It was just a matter of time."

"You anticipated fighting for your Social Gospel."

"That was the case, Marty."

"You couldn't predict that the President would choose that very day to seek a Congressional Resolution to go to war."

"It was the furthest things from my mind when I won office."

President Woodrow Wilson approached the podium to a thunderous applause. Before speaking he seemed nervous. His hands twitched as he shuffled his speech. A vein stood out on his forehead. He took a deep breath and scanned his political peers. For a moment he looked upward, perhaps seeking divine guidance, if not sanction for what he was about to propose. Then he spoke.

WHEREAS, The Imperial German Government has committed repeated acts of war against the people of the United States of America; therefore, be it resolved by the Senate and House of Representatives of the United States of America in Congress assembled, That a state of war between the United States and the Imperial German, which has thus been thrust upon the United States, is hereby formally declared.

WILSON AND WAR

"As I listened to the President I knew my agenda was held hostage to the call for war. I knew in those first moments in Congress that there would be hearings, discussion, and a debate before a final vote. I knew from the cheering that the President would be supported. The loss of what I hoped to accomplish pained me. Domestic policy was being drowned out by the call to arms. The President's claim that war had been 'thrust' upon the United States troubled me. I was unsure about that, since no German soldiers were threatening the Cross Creek Ranch. The daily deadly accounts of the dead on the Western Front horrified me, especially as I thought of Montana's sons."

"History can be fickle, Jean."

"Three days (April 5, 1917) later the House opened debate on the President's War Resolution. Beforehand I spoke with Wellington. My brother urged a yea vote. Many suffrage organizations lobbied me to do the same. Some were concerned that a no vote would show women as weak, or worst yet, unpatriotic."

"You were caught in the middle."

"Of course. As a pacifist I was opposed to war. I also wanted to support my country."

"You listened to the arguments, pro and con?"

"I did and intently. I was much impressed by the speakers and the logic supporting their conclusions."

"You did not participate in the debate, according to the newspapers."

"That was the case."

"And then it was time for a vote?"

"One thing, Jean, before we get to that."

"Yes?"

"What did you know about the war in Europe, especially in 1914 when Europe slid over the ledge?"

"I read the papers. I listed to the news. But the truth is I didn't understand why the death of two people should lead to a war. I didn't understand the jealousies and fear of the European nations. Even more I didn't understand the alliance system and the military preparations that, as I now believe, encouraged war. I was ignorant of the imperialistic designs of the countries involved. I had heard the Balkans were 'a powder keg' ready to explode. I knew there had been trouble in Morocco in North Africa. I knew there were ethnic groups within the Austria-Hungarian Empire that wanted to be free, but in truth my understanding was little."

"Like most Americans?"

"Like most Americans."

"What do you know about the Franco-Prussian War of 1870?"

"Marty, you must be kidding? I was born ten years after Chancellor Otto von Bismarck's war to unite the German states. I was a kid. I was more interested in milking cows and riding horses than Paris feuding with Berlin."

"You knew nothing of France's loss of Alsace-Lorraine?"

"We might as well be talking about Timbuktu."

"You knew the French generals wanted revenge? They wanted those provinces back."

"I knew nothing of that until recently."

"What about the Ottoman Empire, Germany's ally against France?"

"Marty, you continue to probe my ignorance. What did I know? Almost nothing. For me the Ottomans conjectured up images of dashing men in turbans riding on gallant stallions across the desert wastes, brandishing crescent swords."

"Dear lady, do you realize you've raised your voice?"

"I..."

"We must not dispense with our cloak of seclusion."

"Quite right, Marty. We don't want to draw attention to ourselves. But, as you've shown, here I was about to vote on the momentous issue of war, and I knew so little about the European fracas."

"Many of your colleagues were in the same position?"

"Most, I think. We knew what was in the papers. We knew what the President said. We knew what the commentators voiced."

"Some of it was propaganda?"

"Some, perhaps. Other information was tilted one way or another."

"Prejudicial?"

"Certainly."

They paused in their conversation, the older reporter, the younger member of the House... They needed the moment.

"You wanted America to stay out of the war?"

"I saw no value in mass suicide, then or now?"

"Even after the *Lusitania* disaster?"

"That was a terrible moment, such a terrible loss of life."

"After the foolishness of the Zimmerman Note?

"Another terrible blunder by the Imperial German government."

"But not sufficient to go to war, Jean?"

"There had been no direct attack on the United States, Marty."

"That would have pushed you for a war vote?"

"Only that."

"A last question, if I may, Jean?"

"You seem to have many last questions, Marty?"

"What about our nation's honor? Could we let our flag be besmirched by German torpedoes?"

"Honor? What is honor, Marty? Men talk of it and gallantly go off to war. What honor is there in the men entangled in barbed wire, their arms blown off in 'no man's land?' What honor is there in men choking to death from toxic gas? Perhaps because I am a woman, I see none. I am reminded of a few words I picked up somewhere. They are attributed Achilles."

Imagine a king who fights his own battles. Wouldn't that be a sight.

"Wouldn't be easier on all of us, Marty, if the Kaiser and the Czar, and the other royal leaders just fought it out in a closed room instead of sending millions of their subjects to an early grave?"

"You do make a case, Madam. Still, let me push back. Wasn't it Alexander Hamilton, who said, "Those who stand for nothing fall for anything?"

"I am not aware of the quote. All I know is this. I will stand against war and will not be taken in by patriotic exuberance or a press that needs slashing headlines. I will stand or fall on my convictions."

"Let's get back to your vote."

———————

"Yes, the next day, April 6, 1917. I had been in Congress for less than a week. I was now about to vote or whether to send thousands of young men to their deaths."

"A terrible responsibility."

"Marty, all I could see were the faces of young men, and then their weeping mothers and fathers, and sisters, and girlfriends. The images would not retreat from my mind."

"You received letters from the voters?"

"Once elected and with a war vote on the horizon, yes. The mail ran about 16 to 1 against war."

"You divined what from this?"

"The voters shared with me a common view that war was a futile way of solving disputes among nations."

"Some mail attacked you, was that not the case, for your pacifism, claiming that you were weak on foreign policy?"

"That view was misguided. A pacifist can be aggressive in defending the interests of our country, but that doesn't mean acceding to the White House on the issue of war."

"The first roll call was conducted."

"I chose not to vote."

"Then a second roll call came."

"I hesitated. Joseph G. Cannon, a decent man, approached me. Bending down and speaking in hushed terms, he said, 'Little woman you cannot afford not to vote.' Still, I hesitated. He continued, saying, 'You represent the woman of the country in the Congress.' Once more I remained silent. He left with these parting words: 'I shall not advise you how to vote, but you should vote one way or another --- as your conscience dictates.'"

"Your name was called."

"It was."

The Washington Times reported that:

Every eye in the chamber was fixed on you. There was no sound. As you came to a standing position you threw back your head and looked straight ahead. Your hands grasped the back of the seat before you.

"I had to respond. In doing so I inadvertently violated a House Rule when I spoke. I gave a brief speech."

I want to stand by my country, but I cannot vote for war. I vote no.

"You were not alone in your vote."

"That is correct. Fifty members voted nay. The yeas 373 votes."

"But you were the only woman to vote nay."

"I was the only woman in Congress."

"Reaction was swift?"

"Most folks in Montana favored my vote, but not, as usual, the press. The *Helena Independent* likened me to:

> *… a dagger in the hands of the German propagandist, a dupe of the Kaiser, a member of the Hun Army in the US, and a crying school girl.*

A Pittsburgh reporter accused me of 'voting against the flag.' That was painful to hear. He then heaped scorn upon me, commenting on my character. 'Weakness, hesitation, timidity and nervous hysteria were displayed when she should have been strong, courageous and calmly determined.'

"You were nervous?"

"Of course. Who wouldn't be. Casting a vote for war is serious business. And, as to the courage question, of all qualities that was the one I least lacked. It took an iron will to stand by my convictions. It took inner strength to go against the President and the war fever sweeping through the House."

"I heard, Jean, that another reporter declared that you voted 'no' because of your feminine emotions wouldn't permit you to say 'yes' to war."

"I voted as a member of the House. I balanced my convictions with the views of my Montana constituency. Gender played no role.

To suggest otherwise is to express prejudicial views of women in politics. I voted as the women of America knew I would. The NAWSA distanced itself from me, stating that 'Miss Rankin was not voting for the suffragists of the nation --- She represents Montana.' That comment, I must admit, was painful given all the time and effort I had given on behalf of the organization."

"You vote essentially ended your political career?"

"Not necessarily, but it made a reelection run much more difficult."

"You spoke to Wellington?"

"I did."

"He was sympathetic?"

"As a brother, yes. As an astute politician, no."

"You harbor no doubts in your mind as to the vote?"

"None."

"You'll continue to fight for your domestic agenda?"

"Of course. It is my hope to sponsor a suffrage amendment to the constitution."

"And you will support the war effort?"

"I love my country. A decision has been made. I will not desert the young men about to be sacrificed."

"Then you are a patriot?"

"That was never the question, Marty."

There was little to be said now. Jean knew that. Marty knew it. The future await both, Jean in the Congress and Marty and his reporting. As he was about to get up, two women walked over to their table.

"Excuse us, but aren't you Jeannette Rankin?"

"Yes."

"We just wanted to tell you how much we admired your vote. We don't want our sons in that terrible war."

Overhearing this, Marty said, "I think I should take my leave. You ladies, I think, have much to discuss."

With that he gave Jean a smile, and departed into the crowded lobby of the Hotel Mason. As he did, she said, "Take care of yourself Marty."

PART IV

ROBERT LAFOLLETTE

EVERY NATION HAS ITS WAR PARTY... IT IS COMMERCIAL, IMPERIALISTIC, RUTHLESS

BEFORE THE WAR IS ENDED, THE WAR PARTY ASSUMES THE DIVINE RIGHT TO DENOUNCE AND SILENCE ALL OPPOSITION TO WAR AS UNPATRIOTIC AND COWARDLY.

CHAPTER 21

THE SANCTUARY

JANUARY 17, 1919

It was called the Sanctuary. Except for those who worked at the Hotel Mason very few knew about it. It wasn't that it was a secret. Far from that… It just wasn't mentioned to the hotel's patrons, nor was it described in the hotel's literature. Occasionally, a wayward guest inadvertently found his way to it, gazed, and then retreated back into boisterous main lobby where folks congregated. On this particular day two men were in the Sanctuary and it wasn't by chance. An invitation had been given by one and accepted by the other. One of the men was slim and perhaps a little under nourished with a retreating hairline. The other man was tall, robust, the picture of health. He also had a full head of barely manageable hair. Both men had entered the Sanctuary through a side door with a nondescript sign on it: STORAGE.

The two men shook hands before speaking.

"Mr. Marty Cohen?"
"Senator Robert LaFollette?"

"As if they had rehearsed their scripts, they sat down on two wooden Adirondack lounge chairs, the type that were sometimes found along the New England coastline and in the hills of upstate New York. Made of teak the seat of the chairs had a steep slope, while the wooden back slats rose high at a rakish angle. The chairs were just right for these men, both of whom found it difficult to sit for long periods. They simply had too much energy for that. The chairs provided temporary comfort, but that's all.

It was a crisp January morning that not even the morning sun, bright and shining in the heavens, could warm the nation's capital beyond 61 degrees. The two men, of course, were dressed for the occasion --- heavy tweed jackets over warming, wool sweaters. Their pants were heavily lined to ward off the elements. They had dispensed with their hats and had stuffed their thick gloves into their jackets. Heavy scarves no longer encircled their necks.

The smaller of the two men spoke.

"Senator, I ordered hot chocolate and sliced lemon cake to hold us until lunch. I hope that is agreeable."
"Eminently. Used to drink it on the farm. That was a long time ago."
"As a boy?"
"And lemon cake was a favorite of my mother, Mr. Cohen."
"Marty, please."
"I've heard you like that moniker."
"It seems to suit me. Breaks the ice a bit and helps some to warm to me."
"Even on cold morning?"
"Yes, but it might just take a mite longer today."
"And now you'll want to know how to address me?"

"That would be helpful."

"Senator will suffice."

That said the two men were quiet. The Sanctuary seemed to invite quietude. But the two men had come to talk. The silence wouldn't last.

"Marty, it was my understanding that you met Secretary Bryan and Senator Norris in one of the hotel rooms."

"You've been checking up on me."

"Just getting the lay of the land. You met Representative Rankin in the hotel dining room?"

"We did. Delightful lady."

"Then why here for our meeting?"

"To be honest, I needed a diversion. I needed to be outside."

"But why here?"

"I needed to breathe fresh air and smell the sweet fragrance of what is growing."

For the first time, the Senator took in his surroundings. Scattered in a precision manner throughout the Sanctuary were plots of healthy dark earth held in place by large wooden railroad ties. The plots were approximately 6 feet by 10 and arranged to make optimal use of the land available. Growing in the plots, some fifteen in number were strawberries in one, blueberries in another, lettuce here, and tomatoes there. In one plot there were carrots. In another green beans were abundant. In a corner plot, somewhat larger than the others, stalks of corn were struggling to survive. Toward a wooden fence one plot was showered with a staggering array of spring flowers just now bursting forth in color.

"It sort of like a Garden of Eden, Marty."

"About one-half-acre, Senator and without the serpent."

"Reporters don't qualify?"

"Not today, I hope."

"What do you call this place?"

"Unofficially, the hotel refers to it as the Sanctuary."

"Who cares for all this?"

"An old guy. Jake Fields…That's the guy. He used to run the elevator. As I understand it, his wounds and malaria from the war against Spain finally caught up with him. The hotel management didn't want to turn him out. He was given a room and responsibility for cleaning up this outdoor area, which was a mess, a sort of Sargasso Sea full of old boxes containing discarded 'you name it items," plus weeds that were competing with the Amazon Basin. Turns out old Jake had a green thumb. First he cleaned the place up. Then he planted. One thing led to another, as you can see. Turned out to be a good deal for everyone. The hotel staff has a spot for R and R and some of the crops, once harvested, even find themselves into a salad bowl. That should be of interest to you."

"You know?"

"I'm told you're a vegetarian."

"I am."

"Then the lunch salad I ordered will, I hope, appeal to you."

"It will. Where's Jake today?"

"An impromptu day off."

"At your behest, I'm sure, Marty."

Marty Cohen just smiled.

I'm told you always ask one question early on in the interview."

"It is a habit."

"Then ask."

"Senator, why did you finally agree to meet with me? All previous entreaties failed. Why now?"

Senator Robert LaFollette inhaled deeply and then responded with powerful emotions cloaking his words. "Because of what took place yesterday, January 16, 1919."

CHAPTER 22

THE PETITION

"The Senate finally reached a decision, Senator?"

"It did and in my favor."

"After more than a year and a half of what many called a political vendetta?"

"And legal costs to me of over $5000."

"All the charges were dropped?"

"Completely."

"Still, it must have been a painful experience, Sir?"

"I cannot deny that."

"My memory is skimpy on the facts. Indulge me, please. My readers will appreciate the exposition."

"Marty, given the stakes that were involved, they should have the mainly unblemished history. I'm depending on you for that."

"That the mainstream press overlooked?"

"For mainly partisan reasons, yes."

"So you're calling on an old Socialist to set the record straight?"

"As you did for Bryan and Norris, and Miss Rankin."

"Then, proceed.

––––––––––––

"It all began on September 20, 1917. I was he keynote speaker before the Nonpartisan League of Wisconsin. The meeting was held in St. Paul, Minnesota just across the St. Croix River separating the two states. The gathering took place shortly after the Senate supported President Wilson's War Resolution."

"Which you heatedly opposed?"

"That was the case. We'll get to that later. Anyway, in my address to the Nonpartisan League I argued for a number of things dear to my heart and, I thought, important to average folk everywhere. I supported increased taxes on the wealthy, especially during wartime, and because they were outrageously benefitting from war contracts. I also railed against the power of corporations influencing public policy for their own vested interests. Make that greed. In no certain terms I gave a stinging denunciation of America's participation in the war."

"You simultaneously attacked corporate America, the wealthy elite, and the White House."

"That seems to cover the ground, Marty."

"The crowd approved?"

"Sustained cheering and praise."

"But there was a backlash?"

"Almost immediately. The pro-war press in particular thought the speech inappropriate during a national crisis. My speech, as is often the case, was taken out of context. Cherry picking, I believe it is called. My words were distorted to mislead the reader as to what I actually said. Editorials condemned me. Voters wrote harsh letters to me. Many of my Senate colleagues turned away from me."

"And then there was a petition?"

"You know of it?"

"Only slightly."

"The Minnesota Commission of Public Safety took exception to what I said. It filed a petition with the Senate asking that I be expelled from that body."

"An almost unheard of request?"

"And a dangerous precedent to remove a Senator because of his views. How could the Senate debate issues of consequence if that became the norm? Debate would be stifled, would it not, Marty?"

"This was done even though you were a popular Senator and the leader of the Progressive Party in the Senate?"

"Perhaps because of that. The Commission charged that I 'taught disloyalty and sedition,' and that I was 'giving aid and comfort to our enemies.' That baseless attack was, of course, supported by my corporate enemies, the wealthy who liked the present tax laws, and even the President who despised me for my opposition to his war."

"The Senate had been handed a hot potato?"

"Abundantly so. The Senate decided referred the matter to its Committee on Privileges and Elections for review and a recommendation. The issues were, as you might expect, troubling to many Senators. Did I have a right to free speech even during a national emergency? Did the government have the right to censor me? Could my elected position be overturned because of a highly partisan petition?"

"Challenging questions."

"The Committee was chaired by a Wilson supporter who wanted my head. The Committee sent me a questionable copy of my speech made in St. Paul. I was asked if the speech was accurate. It wasn't. It was in fact highly inaccurate. I pointed out that my speech had been extemporaneous. However, an accurate copy of my remarks had been made. The official reporter of the Nonpartisan League had written down every word I said. This copy I sent to the Committee, stating that it was accurate."

"It still contained your inflammatory remarks?"

"It did."

"What happened next?"

"In October I defended myself before the Senate."

CHAPTER 23

THE DEFENSE

"I gave what some called a dramatic speech. My view was straightforward. Free speech is a prerequisite in our society and under our constitution, especially during a crisis. I said:

> The right of the people to discuss the war in all its phases and the right and duty of the people's representatives in Congress to declare the purpose and objects of the war is paramount.

"President Wilson had not stated the 'objects' of the war?"

"No to my satisfaction."

"Making the world 'safe for democracy' was not enough?"

"The goal was appropriate. The means, however, I found wanting, and, of course, there was a paradox."

"Meaning?"

"We're going to war to defend democracy while withholding it to too many people in our own country."

"Blacks and others?"

"Jim Crow?"

"And the women, Marty. Half our population is denied the right to vote."

"Your remarks were well-received?"

"Yes, but only by those opposed to the war. The pro-war contingent denounced me."

"You summed history on your behalf?"

"I did. I pointed out that some of America's greatest political faces had objected to wars in their own time, including Abraham Lincoln, Henry Clay, and Daniel Webster."

"Lincoln?"

"He questioned the need to go to war with Mexico?"

"Webster and Clay?

"Taking on the British in 1812."

"That proved influential, Senator?"

"Sadly, hardly."

"You summarized, I understood, with a key question?"

"During the eight months of the Committee's investigation no one had actually challenged what I said in St. Paul, as to the accuracy of my statements. I asked, 'why was this?' No creditable answer was forthcoming."

"Why was that?"

"The facts were on my side."

"You did have your defenders?"

"Of course. One in particular stated:

*... Whether right or wrong in opposing the declaration of war...
is immaterial. He had a right to his views and he had a right to
express them.*

"Unfortunately, my case dragged on for fourteen months. During that period the pro-war press intensified its criticism. The worst was when he was charged that I justified the sinking of the *Lusitania* back in 1915. That charge was a gross distortion of my views. I had not defended the sinking of that great ship. I did, however, have many questions about the terrible event.

Eventually, the Associated Press notified the Committee that there were inaccuracies in their story. They retracted what they released. It was a backhanded apology of sorts.'

"Which takes us to yesterday, Senator?

"The Committee admitted it found no witnesses to testify against me. Apparently, time had worked in my favor. The war was over. The boys were coming home victors. The President was headed to Europe to remake the world. The public outcry against dissent had run its course. That being the case the Committee recommended that all charges be dismissed, stating that all so-called inflammatory remarks were a matter of debate."

"The Committee, it seemed, wanted to put that chicken to bed."

"No question about that and because of another thing."

"Which was?"

"The more the Committee attacked me the more my popularity soared among the progressive and liberal wings of the Republican Party. The Democrats on the Committee took no delight in that given my interest in running for the White House. The full Senate voted 50 to 21 to exonerate me of all charges. What some thought was a personal vendetta by President Wilson was over."

"What did you think?"

"Censorship is the enemy of free speech. Presidents want an accommodating Congress and a sympathetic public during a national crisis. They strive for unanimity in views that bolster their policies. This desire is magnified ten-fold during wartime."

"Whether President William McKinley in 1898 or Wilson in 1917?"

"That is the case, Marty, as it will be in any future conflict. It is the nature of the beast to restrict our constitutional rights in an emergency. We do so at our own peril."

CHAPTER 24

THE BOUNTY OF
THE LAND

The two men were walking around the Sanctuary, now talking less seriously.

"Look at those raspberries, so reddish and plump. Marty. Do you think anyone would mind?"

"The coast is clear. Go ahead."

Robert LaFollette didn't hesitate. As if my magic into his large hands appeared a plentiful number of raspberries, which he quickly but joyfully ate.

"Delightful. Reminds me of when I was a kid on the farm back in Primrose, Wisconsin. As kids we used for forage for wild berries. If we found enough many ended up in a pie."

"That's where you were born?"

"That was back in 1855. I was the youngest of five children."

"Your parents…"

"My father, Josiah, descended from French Huguenots. My mother, Mary was of Scottish ancestry."

"Quite a combination."

"How about this... My great-grandfather lived in Kentucky. Guess who his neighbor was?"

"I cannot."

"The Lincoln family."

The two men continued their leisurely walk, stopping only when the Senator wanted to sample something."

"That tomato was tangy."

"I'm sure others will find their way into our lunch."

"You're not a vegetarian, Marty?"

"Semi. A sour stomach limits my indulgences."

"A reporter's ailment?"

"An affliction of dealing with Washington politicians, I think."

The two men laughed and moved on to look at the corn.

"Your education, Senator?"

"I'm a University of Wisconsin man. Graduated in 1879 with a Bachelor of Science degree."

"You were a good student?"

"Hardly, but I did excel in oratory contests and, if I recall correctly, I established the first student newspaper on campus, the *University Press*."

"Your first experience with the media?"

"But not, as you know, my last."

"I heard that John Bascom, the university's president, had a powerful influence on your life."

"Indeed he did. He was an excellent scholar and teacher. He was a professor of rhetoric and English literature. And this is important, Marty... He believed the university should exert a strong moral presence. He taught a special course for seniors on the 'importance of using their education to improve society."

"That became important to you?"

"That became my impulse for going into public service."

JOHN BASCOM

The Senator was looking intensely at the corn. A look of disappointment swept over his face.

"Marty, I'm afraid the corn crop will not make it. Probably needs more water and a bit more fertilizer."

"You know corn?"

"Marty, I raised it on the farm and as a politician spewed an occasional bushel."

"It's refreshing to hear a politician who can laugh at himself."

"Do Socialist reporters also do that?"

"Our capitalistic brothers don't often provide that opportunity."

Again, the men strolled, chatting as they went.

"See that, Marty?"

"I'm looking at?"

"This."

The Senator reached into one of the plots and pulled out a handful of soil."

"Dirt."

"No you Socialist. This is America. This is the soil that gave birth to farms across the nation, and hope to hundreds of thousands of families. Soil, Marty, add water and hard, sweaty work and life is reborn. Crops are harvested. A nation is fed. Life continues. That's what this stuff is, our inheritance from the Almighty."

The Senator stopped talking long enough to wipe his hands with a piece of burlap hanging by the less than bountiful corn crop.

"That's America, Marty. Never forget that."

"It appears, Senator, that I have spent too much time walking the hard, concrete sidewalks of our cities."

They walked on. Marty Cohen knew it was time to change the subject.

"Robert, tell me about the Chautauqua circuit."

"You've been doing your homework."

"I understand you lectured on the circuit, giving over 57 speeches in the Mid-west during one particular stint?"

"That many! I guess so. I was always running for something, first to be Governor of Wisconsin, then to find my way into the House of Representatives, and lastly to join the Senate."

"And the White House, Sir?"

"And the White House. Speaking on the circuit was a good way to meet people and establish a reputation based on your views."

"The word Chautauqua meant what?"

"The word was named after a location in New York State and came to mean assemblies. They were very popular in the 1920's, especially in rural and small towns. Usually a big tent was put up near a town --- in a pasture that was well drained, and then speakers showed up: teachers, artists, musicians, showmen, preachers, and entertainers of all sorts."

"Politicians, too?"

"We were part of the entertainment. Did you known that Secretary Bryan also hit the circuit. Made quite a name for himself on it."

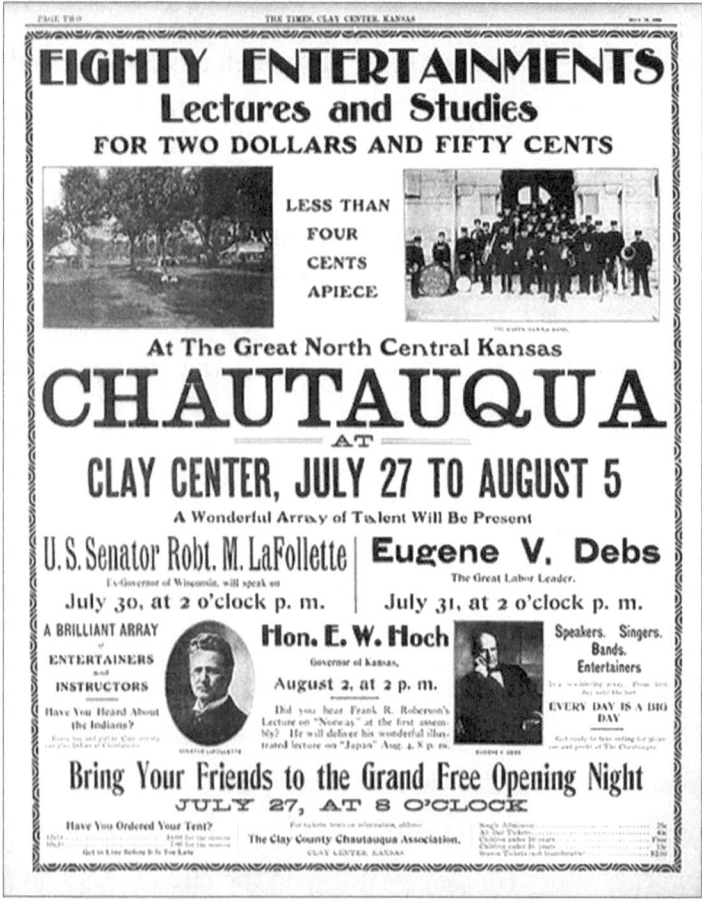

THE BIG TENT

"The speeches you gave honed your political views?"

"My progressive views evolved over time. Basically, I stood for:

- the implementation of primary elections.
- the direct election of Senators.
- reforming the tax system to make it fairer.
- regulating the railroads.
- regulating utilities.
- breaking the power of monopolies
- providing cheap credit to famers.
- ending child labor by law.
- supporting labor unions.
- protecting civil liberties.
- a national referendum to stop Presidents from going to war.
- the right of citizens to recall a politician
- the right to place a proposition on the ballot.

"That's quite a laundry list, Senator."

"I guess old man Bascom got to me."

"And you got to the voters?"

"I tried."

The two men headed back to their seat, one nourished by nature's bounty, the other, as always, wanting more information. It was time to move on again and Marty Cohen knew that.

"Sir, you mentioned the *Lusitania*. It would like to go back to that with your permission?"

QUESTIONS

"Let's get this straight before we start. Marty, I never justified what happened to the *RMS Lusitania*. I never took the side of Berlin in the ensuing debate about the wanton sinking of a cruise ship. I merely asked uncomfortable questions the Administration wanted to avoid. I only raised issues the pro-war press wanted ignored. No more, no less."

"Still, there were those who felt you were unpatriotic?"

"Unfortunately, yes. In wartime there is a push toward conformity in thinking and action. We've already discussed that. Criticism of government policy is not desired. The wide discussion of controversial issues is always a victim of wartime censorship. That's what got me into trouble."

"No regrets?"

"Only one. I wished I had been more successful."

"Interesting that you would say that. Secretary Bryan and Miss Rankin felt the same way, as did Senator Norris about their efforts to stop Wilson's drift toward war."

"All peas in the same pod, it seems. That said, let's get on with it, Marty."

"As you wish Senator. The facts, as I understand them, are these. The facts are these. On May 7, 1915 the British liner, the *RMS*

Lusitania, was torpedoed by the *U-20* at 2:00 p.m. eleven miles off the southern coast of Ireland. At that precise time and location the ship was in a war zone defined by German blockade of Great Britain. Aboard the *Lusitania* were 1,266 passengers and 696 crewmembers, a total of 1,962 souls. Of that number 1,198 died including women and children. There were 48 large lifeboats aboard the ship. However, because of the severe list, only 6 lifeboats were successfully launched. Once torpedoed the *Lusitania* went down in 18-minutes. It was the 202nd second crossing of the Atlantic for the cruise ship and its last. Those are the facts."

"But not the complete story, Marty."

THE RMS LUSITANIA

"You're getting at what, Senator?"

"The ship was traveling under what were called Cruiser Rules. According to the Declaration of Paris in 1915 and before war zones and blockades were established by Germany and Britain these rules were to govern ships at sea. They specifically codified the rules of engagement involving civilian vessels. The details were these. The passengers and crew had to be safeguarded before a ship was sunk. This, of course, was not done in the case of the *Lusitania*. The civilian ship also had responsibilities, including these: first it had to fly its own flag. It could not sail under false colors to avoid a confrontation. It could not pretend to be a different nationality. The British flag flew in the yardarms of the *Lusitania*. There was no question about that. Second, the civilian ship had to stop when confronted. This occurred. Third, the civilian ship had to allow boarding by a search party. This never happened. The surprise torpedo attack precluded that. Fourth, the civilian ship could not take evasive tactics. The *Lusitania* never had time for this. Finally, the civilian ship could not be armed nor could it attempt to ram a submarine."

"But you had questions?"

"Indeed, first and foremost, why was the ship bearing contraband produced in the United States when our policy was strict neutrality? Were we violating our own stated policy? Second, why were Americans aboard a ship heading into dangerous waters? Third, since the British Admiralty helped design the ship and the *Lusitania* sailed under orders of the Admiralty was the *Lusitania* in actuality a naval vessel? Fourth, did the Captain have secret orders to ram any German submarine it encountered, as many have suggested? These questions occurred to me."

"What about the infamous German warning?"

"You speak of the notification put out by the Imperial German Embassy in New York?"

THE WARNING

"I do."

"Marty, the warning was placed in fifty American newspapers by the German Imperial Government. It was printed next to the Cunard advertisement indicating when the *Lusitania* would leave Pier 54 at 12:20 p.m. on May 1915 out of New York City. The NOTICE explicitly warned Americans to avoid sailing on this ship heading into a war zone. The implication was clear. Americans would be traveling at their own risk if they did so. Many Americans were not deterred by the warning and 128 of them died."

"Even before the sinking you questioned the right of Americans to travel on belligerent ships."

"I did. American citizens on such ships were an incident waiting to happen. It was just a matter of time."

"President Wilson supported their right to travel?"

"He did, but he was not unaware of the risks. The pro-war faction in his administration, some might argue, considered an 'incident,' however, a necessity in getting the country into the war."

"That is a strong indictment."

"It is."

"Wilson was caught between a nation unprepared for war and those clamoring for a conflict, Senator?"

"He was. The American press was fueling public anger, claiming the German government was guilty of mass murder.

The New York Times.

LUSITANIA SUNK BY A SUBMARINE, PROBABLY 1,000 DEAD;
TWICE TORPEDOED OFF IRISH COAST; SINKS IN 15 MINUTES;
AMERICANS ABOARD INCLUDED VANDERBILT AND FROHMAN;
WASHINGTON BELIEVES THAT A GRAVE CRISIS IS AT HAND

"Marty, on May 13. 1915 the President emphatically 'upheld the indisputable right of American citizens to sail the high seas.' He demanded the German government disavowed the blockade policy and asked for reparation for damages. The German government, as was expected, stated that the *Lusitania* was no ordinary unarmed civilian vessel. She was carrying munitions in her hold."

"That was the case, wasn't it?"

"The ship was carrying 4200 cases of small arms, some 173 tons in total weight, guns and ammunition."

"The press, however, was not concerned about a technicality."

"Marty, the *New York Times* demanded that Germany shall no longer make war like savages drunk with blood.' The *New York Nation* summed up many views:

> To speak of technicalities and the rules of war in the face of such wholesale murder on the high seas, is a waste of time. The law of nations and the law of God have been alike trampled upon. The torpedo that sank the Lusitania also sank Germany in the opinion of mankind. It is at once a crime and a monumental folly. She has affronted the moral sense of the world and sacrificed her standing among the nations.

"Heeding the public's anger the President sent a second note to Germany on June 9, 1915 that moved the country closer to war. Wasn't that the case, Senator?"

"Yes and so much so that Secretary of State Bryan resigned from the Cabinet. Wilson was preparing to arm our merchant ships in defense of freedom of the seas. Bryan felt such a policy would of necessity lead to another incident and further aggressive notes to Berlin. Bryan was right and I agreed with him. Senator Norris, as you know, also felt this way. And, of course, Miss Rankin's vote reflected her views. Arming our ships while permitting them to sail into hostile waters flew in the face of strict neutrality. Continuing to offer loans to the British and to ship munitions only added to an already combustible situation. These were the stands I took in my increasing determination to avoid war. What the *U-20* did was horrendous. What we were doing was not helpful."

"Much of this history you spoke to in your St. Paul speech."

"Yes, Marty, and that brings us full circle, does it not?"

"It does but first lunch and then I'll sidetrack you for a moment before we get to your fateful speech in the Senate in opposition to the President."

"You do have a way with words, Marty."

CHAPTER 26

THE TELEGRAM

The two men were enjoying their lunch. A beautiful glass bowl was before them on a small table fitted with a spanking white tablecloth. The large bowl contained, it seemed a bounty of crisp lettuce, carrots, tomatoes, green onions, sliced cucumbers, both green and red peppers, kernels of corn, a sample of green peas, and splendid little lumps of hard boiled eggs. Off to the side was a smaller bowl containing the hotel's special salad dressing that contained imported Italian olive oil. On another plate was an ordered pile of bread sticks, still warm from the oven. As would be expected two exquisite salt and pepper dispensers were on the table. The hotel bragged they were imported from Japan. Two large plates with the hotel's monogram on them were also on the table, along with the usual utensils. A large pitcher of ice tea and two tall greenish-colored glasses were also on the table. And lastly, there was a small basket of fresh fruit to complete the lunch picture."

"The hotel staff has been busy, Marty."
"And discrete, Senator. Shall we?"

The two men sat down and ate their lunch, only stopping at times to make what some might call "small talk."

"Marty, a question for you."

"Senator?"

"You're a Socialist."

"My pedigree."

"You support Socialist candidates?"

"Of course."

"Who have great difficult in winning elections?"

"Except for a few local elections that is the case."

"You sense no futility in this?"

"None, and before you ask, the reason is this. We're winning."

If the Senator was caught off guard by Marty's declaration, he disguised his feelings, only saying, "You will explain."

"Senator, you belong to the Progressive wing of the Republican Party. From the perspective of a Socialist, your wing has co-opted many issues dear to my Socialist heart. Recall your laundry list. You want to break the power of monopolies. So do Socialists. You want social and economic justice. So do Socialists. You are opposed to child labor. You support labor's right to organize. Again, so do Socialists. You stand for suffrage. You weigh in against unregulated railroads, banks, and utilities. So do Socialists. In many cases we Socialists were for these things before others adopted these positions. True in some situations we would go further, but that is of no great import. What is important is this. We would both use the power of government to improve the lives of ordinary people."

"And when it comes to war, Marty?"

"We tend to be pacifists. That you know. That, however, doesn't mean we're against all wars. We are simply unwilling to enter a war that benefits the rich at the expense of the poor, but you know that."

"A position I have also taken."

"Then we are brothers, are we not?"

The question hung in the air as the men finished their meal. Always the instigator, Marty moved on with his questioning.

"Senator, as I recall you got into some difficulty over the Zimmerman Telegram?"

"I did."

"Let's talk about that."

"If you must."

"Senator, the facts seem to be these. On March 27, 1917, Arthur Zimmerman told the German Reichstag that a certain telegram was 'genuine.' He further stated that he had sent that telegram. It was a secret message to Heinrich von Eckardt, the German ambassador to Mexico. We are in agreement so far?"

"Yes."

"The secret coded message was sent in anticipation of a renewal of unrestricted submarine warfare by Germany. It was understood by Berlin that the resumption would most probably bring America into the war. It was, it appeared, a gamble the German military was willing to take. Wilson, the German government concluded, would have no choice. For all intents and purposes it amount to a declaration of war. The German military assumed it would take close to a year before America could draft, train, and transport an expeditionary force to the Western Front. With Russia knocked out of the war, Germany felt she could defeat the French and British armies before the Yanks arrived."

"That seems to cover it, Marty."

"The secret telegram was intercepted by the British, who later released it to the American news press. The British hoped that disclosure of the telegram's contents would hasten America's entry into the war. You recall, don't you, Senator, what was disclosed?"

"I do. In the event the United States entered the war, Germany would form an alliance with Mexico, and assist that country in recapturing Texas, New Mexico, and Arizona. Beyond funding, how this was to be accomplished was not explained."

"The headlines burned with the disclosure of a secret treaty?"

"They did, Marty."

"The British disclosure and the blistering headlines had the desired effect. Americans turned against Germany. War fever was reaching an uncontrolled pitch."

"Still, you resisted getting caught up in the frenzy of anti-Mexican anger and the German promise to resume "the ruthless employment of their submarines."

"I did and with good reason. First, the threat of an alliance was a hollow gesture on the part of Berlin. It was a clumsy way to sidetrack the United States. Already occupied with the European Conflict, there was no way Germany could assist Mexico City in regaining territories lost in the 1848 Mexican War. Second, rather than diverting

America's attention from assisting the British, the telegram had the opposite effect. The political editorials made sure of that."

"Yet, you still resisted going to war?"

"My reasoning was this. The Europeans were almost done. They had been killing each other for years. Millions were dead and wounded. The European economies were bankrupt. Soldiers were mutinying. Revolutionary groups were seeking to overthrow ancient aristocracies. The Czar had fallen in Russia. The Ottoman Empire was in collapse. The Hapsburgs were discredited in Vienna. The Kaiser himself was under pressure to abidicate. The bloody mess was coming to an end."

"But Germany might still win with a last advance?"

"Possibly, but not probable. And what would she win, some sort of negotiated end to the hostilities?"

"The war was ending?"

"The old men making war were running out of young bodies. Yes, it was ending. Paradoxically, our possible entry only encouraged London and Paris to continue fighting. Remember, they wanted more than an end to the war. They wanted a victor's peace with Germany destroyed as a commercial and military power. To that extent the Zimmermann Telegram was a priceless piece of propaganda. It pushed public opinion over the abyss. These thoughts I tried to convey to others. As events proved, I was running against the tide."

"You have a last aside, Marty?"

"I do. The Espionage Act of 1917."

CHAPTER 27

CIVIL LIBERTIES AT STAKE

"Senator, you were opposed to the Espionage Act of 1917?"

"I was. I was also opposed to additional provisions to the Act."

"As, I might add, were Socialists."

"The Act prohibited interference with any and all military operations or recruitment."

"It was also supposed to prevent insubordination in the military."

"Marty, the Act was wide enough in its interpretation that any action might be construed a support for an enemy."

"That, of course, was the great danger. Civil liberties could be curtailed, even eliminated under martial law. The President was aware of these dangers, Senator?"

"Yes. However, he believed that censorship was absolutely necessary for the public safety during a national emergency."

"Some was needed?"

"Some, Marty."

"It was now a crime, however, to convey information with 'intent to interfere with the operation or success of the armed forces of the United States. This was punishable by death or by imprisonment for not more than 30-years. It was also a crime to convey false reports or false statements with intent to interfere with the operation of the military forces. It was a crime to cause insubordination, disloyalty, mutiny, and refusal of duty in the armed forces of the United States. All this was punishable by a maximum fine of $10,000 or by imprisonment for not more than 20-years."

"The Act, Marty, also permitted the Postmaster General to impound or to refuse to mail publications that 'he determined were in violation of its prohibitions.'"

"Regardless of the intent the government, by law, was attempting to control free speech when it came to wartime preparations. This became abundantly clear on May 16, 1918 when the law was extended by the Sedition Act of that year. The additional provisions prohibited many forms of speech including 'any disloyal, profane, scurrilous, or abusive language about the form of government of the United States or the flag of the United States, or the uniform of the United States.'"

"What you say is true, Marty."

"We were going to war to make 'the world safe for democracy' while curtailing constitutional rights at home?"

"Truly, an irony."

"You are aware, are you not, Marty, of the furor over the film, *The Spirit of '76?*"

"I must plead ignorance."

"The producer Robert Goldstein, a Jew of German origins, was prosecuted under the Sedition Act. The government seized the film on the grounds that it depicted cruelty on the part of British soldiers during the American Revolution. It was determined that the film would undermine support for our new wartime ally."

"But the British were cruel?"

"You're missing the point on purpose, I think."

"There you have me, Senator."

"What about Tom Watson, the southern populist?"

"Never heard of him."

"Marty, he was an opponent of the draft and the war among other things. The postmasters in Savannah, Georgia and Tampa, Florida refused to mail his publication called the *Jeffersonian*. Watson sought an injunction against the postmasters. The case came before a federal judge. The judge called his publication 'poison' and denied his request. The postmasters were essentially censoring free speech."

"Senator, let me ask you this. You've heard of the Socialist monthly entitled *The Masses*?"

"Marty, now I have to confess my ignorance."

"The postmaster in New York refused the mails to the publisher, citing the 'general tenor.'"

"Which could mean almost anything in the eyes of censors."

"That is, of course, the slippery slope of censorship. Where does it end?"

"That is why I opposed the Sedition Act."

"If you will bear with me, Senator, another example of the treacherous slopes comes to mind --- the case concerning the Watch Tower Bible and Tract Society's publication of the book, *Preachers Present Arms*."

"That case I knew well. The officers of the Society were charged with attempting to cause insubordination, disloyalty, refusal of duty in the armed forces and obstructing the recruitment and enlistment service of the US while it was at war. The government threw the whole book at the Society."

"What was the offending passage that caused the problem?"

"As I recall, Marty…

Nowhere in the New Testament is patriotism encouraged.
Everywhere and always murder in its every form is forbidden.
And yet under the guise of patriotism civil governments of the
earth demand of peace-loving men in the sacrifice of themselves
and their loved ones and the butchery of their fellows, and hail it
as a duty demanded by the laws of heaven.

"The directors were sentenced to 20 years' imprisonment. They served nine months in the Atlanta Penitentiary before being released on bail at the order of Supreme Court Justice Louis Brandeis."

"I think we've exhausted the issue, Marty. I opposed censorship and the curtailment of civil liberties, even during a national emergency. I still do. Let's move on."

CHAPTER 28

THE SPEECH

"The background to your speech, Senator, if you will…"

"It was April 2, 1917 and the scene was very dramatic. President Wilson was calling for war, stating that the United States must 'fight to defend the rights of small nations, to make the world safe for democracy, to establish global peace.' Quoting Martin Luther, the President said, 'God helping us, we can do no other.'"

"Powerful words…"

"The President added:

> Germany had plunged the world into a new dark age. The United States alone, possessed the power and the moral idealism to bring the war to an honorable and just conclusion or the ultimate peace of the world and for the liberation of its peoples.

"The Congress, of course, exploded into applause. Senators shouted, clapped, waved flags, and in a few cases even wept. I was one of few who did not join in the rejoicing. I sat silently in my seat with my arms folded across my chest."

"By remaining seated you took your stand."

"As always, you do have a way with words. The next day, the Senate Foreign Relations Committee introduced a resolution to declare war on Germany. It was assumed that the Senate vote would be unanimous."

"You changed all that?"

"I objected to unanimous consideration."

"This set off a fire storm?"

"It meant a vote would be postponed for a full day. The Senate rules required this in order to avoid hasty votes on significant topics of public concern. My colleagues were not happy about this. They wanted to get on with the business of war."

"Tell me about the rope incident."

"Marty, on the way back to my office someone handed me a rope, suggesting, I assume, that I might meet a traitor's death."

"Emotions were running high."

"Indeed. On April 4, 1917 at 4:00 p.m. I rose to speak. It was my opportunity to spell out why I was opposed to war. The President had spoken for 36-minutes. I would take slightly longer to make my points."

———————

"I began my speech with an ominous warning. There was a dangerous trend in the country to stand by the President without inquiring whether he was right or wrong."

"A concern shared by Socialists, believe me, Senator."

"I pointed out that I didn't subscribe to that doctrine and I never would. I continued:

I shall support the President in the measures he proposes when I believe them to be right. I shall oppose measures proposed by the President when I believe them to be wrong. The fact of the matter which the President submits for consideration is of the greatest importance is only an additional reason why we should be sure that we are right and not to be swerved from that conviction or intimidating in its expression by any influence of its power whatsoever."

"You touched on a sensitive issue, had you not?"

"When Wilson was Governor of New Jersey, he was criticized openly by the Republicans. Even disgruntled members of the Democratic Party did so at times. When he became President the chorus of nays followed him into the White House. All that was to be expected. That was the democratic process at work concerning most issues. However, when it came to war somehow the Commander and Chief was infallible. He was above reproach when it came to a Declaration of War. The Congress fell into lockstep. Debate was muted. Support for the President was demanded."

"You saw the flaws in this approach?"

"I did. Presidents can be wrong."

"But to attack President Wilson on this issue, was that not dangerous to your political fortunes?"

"It was. I had to choose principle over political pragmatism? I knew no other way to honestly represent the people of Wisconsin regardless of the political implications."

"You stood by your convictions in your speech?"

"I stated that the President was not only wrong but also deceptive in his justification for war. He had claimed the cause of democracy as the supreme end of America's war policy. That claim, however, was open to debate. The British, it is fair to say, cared little about the plight of Ireland, Egypt, or India. I pointed out that millions languished under British rule in undemocratic servitude in these countries. As to France, Italy, and Russia, all allies of the British, they still sought to maintain their empires. Preserving democracy was important, but not limited to France and Great Britain."

"Senator, weren't we, I submit, guilty of the same things? We had reaped an empire as a result of the Spanish-American War. We controlled Cuba, Puerto Rico, Guam, and the Philippines. Regardless of what we called it, we were now an imperialistic power."

"Now about to fight on behalf of our fellow imperialists. As I told my colleagues, we are uniting with Great Britain, an empire founded upon the conquests and subjugation of weaker nations."

"Ironic, wasn't it?"

The Senator stopped talking. He seemed to be collecting himself before moving on.

"I tried to explain the origins of the European War as I saw it. Why were the Europeans consciously destroying their own civilization? Simplistic or not, my answer was this. Commercial rivalries and imperialistic ambitions were at the bottom of the whole business."

"What about opportunistic politicians and powerful business interests?"

"Marty, some saw war as an opportunity for profit and power for themselves. These men were wholly indifferent to the suffering they knew war would bring. They were motivated by greed. They were amoral to the core."

"You then took on the question of the infamous war zones and naval blockades?"

"I pointed out that our failure to treat all belligerent nations with the strictest neutrality was the cause of our current situation. We had not rejected the war zones equally. We accepted the British surface blockade and decried the German submarine blockade. Both blockades were illegal. In the process of doing this we have inflamed the mind of our people into a frenzy for war. We have made a mockery of our neutrality policies by allowing Britain to take advantage of it because of her sea power. We have permitted the British to stop shipments of food and medicine to Germany, knowing full well the harm this would cause. In this sense we were an ally of Britain long before Wilson's war resolution."

"You then posed a most interesting question before the Senate?"

"I asked the Senate to put the question to the American people. Why not have a national referendum, one way or another? Let the American people decide since they would have to do the fighting and dying?"

"The Senate gave no credence to your offer?"

"I don't believe the Senate trusted the American people? A vote might be for peace. No referendum was permitted."

"And then you were done?"

"Patience, Marty. I shared with the Senate two last thoughts.

Should we to maintain the technical right of travel and the pursuit of commercial profit, hurl this country into the bottomless pit of the European horror? The laboring men do not want to go to war. They have nothing to sell but their lives. The enemy is not in Germany but on Wall Street.

————————

"I stopped speaking at 6:45 p.m. There were, according to many, tears streaming down my cheeks. Some said I looked like a 'despairing man who had failed to keep his child from doing itself irreparable harm.' I then slumped down into my seat and closed my eyes."

————————

The men stood and slowly walked through the Sanctuary one more time. It was time to leave, but it was apparent they were reluctant to leave this place of peace.

"You will continue fighting, Senator?"

"For what I believe, yes. And you, Marty?"

"I'll write and try to stay a few steps ahead of the federal agents I fear are closing in on me."

"One way or another, I'm sure you'll survive."

BOOK 2

CONFLICT IN SOUTHEAST ASIA

Unlike the Japanese attack on Pearl Harbor it is difficult to know when the Vietnam War began. Some would argue it began in 1919 in Paris when a young man wanted to present a petition to President Woodrow Wilson. His name was Nguyen Tat Than. He was a kitchen assistant at the Ritz Hotel. He was also a Vietnamese patriot who wanted his country free of French colonial control. History would later know this man by his adopted name, Ho Chi Minh. His petition was ignored. During the next half century he would continue the struggle for Vietnam independence, first against French colonial power, later against Japanese aggressors, then the French again after World War II, and lastly against the United States in the 1960's. Had President Wilson granted the audience and accepted the petition how different history might have been in in Southeast Asia.

HO CHI MINH

Did the conflict begin the late 1940's when President Harry S. Truman authorized US financial support of the French effort to reestablish their colonial control over Indo-China, including the areas of Cambodia, Laos, and Vietnam? Had the French not clung to their colonial possessions, there would have been no need for even this tepid involvement by Washington. Or did the war begin in 1954 when President Dwight D. Eisenhower refused to commit American troops to Vietnam during and immediately after the battle of Dien Bien Phu when French troops were defeated by North Vietnam forces? That victory by Ho Chi Minh's troops split the country. The French retreated to South. Ho controlled the North.

Perhaps, as some historians suggest, the Geneva Accords in 1954 laid the groundwork for a future deadly conflict in Southeast Asia. The "Accords" were hammered out in Switzerland between April 26, 1954 and July 20, 1954. They attempted to stabilize the situation in Vietnam by providing the French with an honorable process by which they would relinquish their colonial possessions. Seventy-five years of French colonialism would end. The "Accords" also provided a framework for the eventual reunification of the country. If implemented successfully, the fighting between the Communist North and the more democratic South would end. The key provisions were as follows:

- Vietnam would be divided into two areas by a provisional military demarcation line running along the 17th parallel. The division would last for two years. The demarcation line would separate contending military forces. A demilitarize zone would be established on each side of the line. Temporary governments would exist on either side of the 17th parallel.
- Free general elections by secret ballot would be held in July 1956 under the supervision of an International Supervisory Commission. The election would determine the political system and government in a newly independent and reunited Vietnam. This process was in line with the generally accepted American policy of "self-determinism" first enunciated by President Woodrow Wilson in his famous Fourteen Points.

The Communist North Vietnam government signed the agreement. France, China, the Soviet Union, and the United Kingdom also signed off. The non-Communist government South rejected the agreement. The United States did not sign. Washington took "note" of the ceasefire agreements and stated it "would refrain from the threat or use of force to disturb them." This equivocal position by the Eisenhower Administration, many later thought, suggested the United States would only accept an election outcome in line with its emerging Cold War policy in Southeast Asia. In short, an election victory by Ho Chi Minh's communist government was unacceptable

Some contend that the questionable "Domino Theory" all but made war inevitable. The idea was that "if one country in Southeast Asia fell to the communists, the entire region, much like a line of dominos, would fall and the ripple effects would be felt throughout the Asia-Pacific world." (see map, next page) Dean Rusk, the Assistant Secretary of State, made the argument this way in 1951:

> It is generally acknowledged that if Indochina were to fall...Burma and Thailand would follow sit almost immediately. Therefore, it would be difficult, if not impossible for Indonesia, India, and the others to remain outside the Soviet-dominated Asian Bloc.

In 1964 Secretary of Defense Robert McNamara stated the case as follows with reference to Vietnam"

> We seek an independent non-Communist South Vietnam. Unless w can achieve this objective... almost all of Southeast Asia will probably fall under Communist dominance.

The "domino theory" supported two American policies at the outset of the Cold War. The first policy was called "containment." It was predicated on keeping Communism where it existed, namely the Soviet Union and Mainland China. This policy was utilized during the Korean War in 1950. North Korea aggressors would be pushed back across the 38th parallel, the line that divided the country. The second policy was deterrence. The potential use of atomic weapons symbolized and expressed the determination of the United States to halt the expansion of Red Russia or Communist China.

If the "domino theory" was accepted and acted upon, two things would come to pass. First, free elections in Vietnam would not be supported by the United States because Ho Chi Minh, the popular patriot and nationalist in the North, would win. Second, the United States would have to prop up the South Vietnamese government financially and militarily if the country entered into a civil war, and that raised the question about the use of American land forces in Southeast Asia.

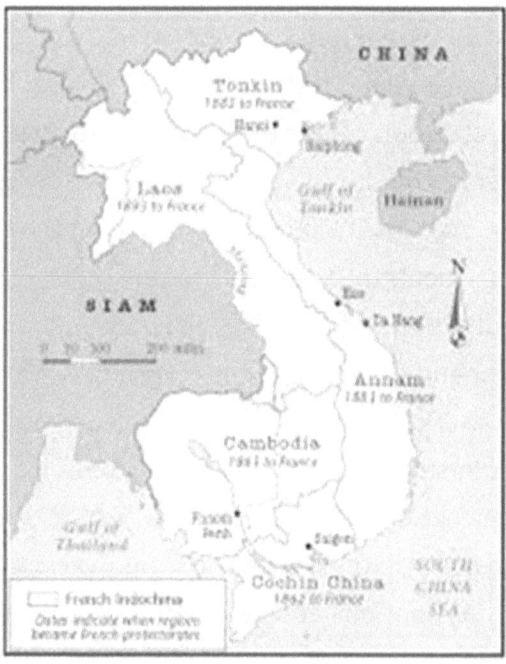

By the 1960's, given this potential situation, alarm bells were going off in Washington, rung mainly by Defense Secretary, Robert McNamara under John F. Kennedy and his successor, Lyndon B. Johnson. In 1963 the Secretary warned that "unless the current trends are reversed in the next two or three months it is likely a communist-controlled state will emerge" in Vietnam. He added, "there is no organized government in South Vietnam" and that "the Viet Cong were winning the war." He recommended that the United States must "intervene" on behalf of the South, and that this was a "test" of American leadership." Failure to act, he stated, would be "damaging to American prestige" around the world." The Johnson administration accepted this thesis. American ground troops would be sent to Vietnam. Eisenhower's cautious approach was thrown to the wind. Vietnam was now seen as a proxy war between the United States and the Soviet Union with Communist China lurking on the sidelines.

On August 5, 1964, President Johnson requested the authority for the use of conventional forces in Southeast Asia. He did not ask for a formal declaration of war by the Congress. Rather, he wanted a resolution permitting him to do whatever was necessary to assist South Vietnam. As a justification for this request the President cited two naval engagements in the Gulf of Tonkin off the North Vietnam coast. Reportedly, the attacks involved the *USS Maddox* on August 2nd and the *Maddox* and the *USS C. Turner Joy* on the 4th. The President contended the attack by North Vietnam PT boats was "unprovoked" and in international waters. Later it was determined the two ships were conducting electronic intelligence missions. On August 7, 1964 the Congress acceded to the President's request. Less than nine hours of committee deliberations and floor debate took place before the

Tonkin Gulf Resolution was approved. The President now had a free hand. He could act as he felt necessary. Some referred to this power as a "blank check."

USS C. TURNER JOY

Only two Senators voted against the Tonkin Gulf Resolution. One was Senator Wayne Morse of Oregon. The other was Senator Ernest Gruening of Alaska. Why did they oppose the President and not side with a majority of the Senate? Why did they accept the harsh criticism they knew would result from their vote? Why did they jeopardize their political futures by sailing against the prevailing winds? These questions will be the focus of the next chapters.

PART V

THE DESSENTING DUO

SENATOR WAYNE MORSE   SENATOR ERNEST GRUENING

DISSENT IS THE HIGHEST FORM OF PATRIOTISM
HOWARD ZINN

CHAPTER 29

INHERITANCE – 1973

Let's be clear about one thing from the start. My name is Rachel Bloom and I had no intention of writing an anti-war book. It's true I'm a somewhat successful writer of romance novels. Perhaps you've read one of my intrusions into the fictionalized lives of women --- *Love in the Shadows, A Ring for Marie,* or *The Clock Continues to Tick.* While my literary efforts never made the *New York Times* "top ten list," they did pay the bills, permitting me to live a comfortable middle class life in Seattle, Washington. I live with two wonderful roommates on 12th Avenue S in a rented house overlooking Interstate 5, the Port of Seattle, and the waters of Puget Sound. One roommate, Margo, is a fashion designer and part time model. My other companion is Joyce. She's a nurse who works for the local Kaiser Hospital. She deals with cancer patients. I don't know how she does it.

As I said, I never thought I'd get deeply involved writing an anti-war book. History was never my thing. In high school I passed my US History class, but it was a little like taking Cod Liver Oil. In the US Government class I listened, completed my assignments, and earned a B grade. I really didn't get into that current event stuff or political debates. It wasn't that I wasn't interested. It was just that I was more interested in other things, mainly literature, poetry, and writing. When I attended Washington State, the same afflictions followed me. There I earned a BA in American Literature. Later I matriculated to the University of Washington, where I earned an MA in English. Then it was off to the real world. I tried teaching in the Seattle public schools. I liked the kids. I didn't like grading essays or the petty school politics. I moved on. Eventually, I found my calling, romance novels. Who would have guessed?

This whole anti-war business all started with a letter from Jenkins and Jenkins, a New York City legal firm. Apparently, I was a very distant descendent of Marty Cohen. I had heard his name mentioned a few times at family gatherings but only in passing and with little exposition. What did I know about him? He was a reporter working for a Socialist newspaper eons ago. He interviewed members of the government during the presidency of Woodrow Wilson. That was all back in 1917. That was it.

As I was told by Jenkins and Jenkins, a Professor of History, Myron Simmons, wanted to contact me about this relative. Simmons, who was in poor health, needed my help in completing a book about Cohen. He knew I was a writer. He knew I was a distant relative. That's what sent him in my direction.

At first I was unimpressed by Simmons' overture, but I must admit, I was curious. I reached out to the professor. We talked. He sent me everything he had on this Marty Cohen, all of which I read. His interview with Secretary of State, William Jennings Bryan caught my attention. To resign from a powerful political office, so hard to believe... The interviews with the senators, Norris and LaFollette really got to me. I was "hooked." I agreed to help Simmons. The book, if published, would bear both our names. Somewhere in the back of my mind, I thought, my old high school history teacher must have been laughing.

My task was to interview two former US Senators, Wayne Morse from Oregon and Ernest Gruening from Alaska. I was to focus on their opposition to President Lyndon Johnson's Tonkin Gulf Resolution, which he had submitted to the Senate for passage. Since the two men were in ill health there was some urgency in this matter. I contacted them, and after considerable discussion, they agreed to meet. We did so. What follows are the highlights of our conversations.

One other point... When I asked them why they agreed to meet, they said, "Young woman, Marty Cohen is our hero, forgotten and ignored by most, but a brave soul who spoke out against war." It would take me some time before I would appreciate their praise.

CHAPTER 30

THE OREGONIAN

I first met with Wayne Morse in his home in Eugene, Oregon. Though he had a reputation as being feisty, cantankerous, and without humor, I found him to be most agreeable and friendly. We began with his years before Tonkin Gulf.

"I was born in Madison, Wisconsin on October 20, 1900. I was a new baby for a new century. My father was Wilbur F. Morse. My mother was Jessie Elnoa. Together they owned and ran a 300-acre farm. They raised kids, of course, plus dairy cows, hogs, sheep, poultry, and crops for the animals. It was hard work. They didn't complain. I learned not to. At dinner we had family discussions about politics, education, religion, and farming. All the kids were expected to join in. I did. I learned to defend myself against an onslaught of opposing ideas."

"Good training for politics?"

"It was, Miss Bloom."

"Rachel, please."

"Okay. We were good Republicans. Our hero was, as you might expect, "Fighting Bob LaFollette." He was our kind of progressive politician. He was always fighting for the guy on the street."

"Your schooling?"

"I started out in a two-room rural classroom. My parents believed in education. They sent me to the Longfellow School in Madison. It was a 22-mile round trip journey each day by horseback. "

"You do well?"

"I guess so. I certainly learned how to ride a horse."

"College?"

"The University of Wisconsin. I graduated in 1923 with a BA. Stayed a while longer and got an MA in speech. I then crossed the state line and attended the University of Minnesota Law School. I finished in 1928."

"You taught?"

"You've done your research, Rachel. Yes, I taught law at the University of Oregon and at the age of 31 I became the Dean of the Law School."

"And that made you the youngest law school dean in the country."

"It did."

"In time you entered politics?

"A rewarding but challenging line of work."

"Sir, what were your core values?"

"Traditional Republicans values motivated me. I believed in a thrifty government. I believed in small government. I accepted the need for a strong military."

"But you also challenged your party and absolute obedience to these thresholds?"

"Where government action was necessary, I was for it. If funds needed to be appropriated for a worthy public cause, I was in favor of the legislation. As to a strong military, the size and scope of the armed forces was never the problem. My concern had to do with the 'when' and 'how' the troops would be deployed."

"Especially if the United States hadn't been physically attacked?"

"That was for me always the heart of the matter. As you know, I took a few hits on that one."

"The Senate can be a place of hard knocks?"

"Especially when you're in the minority, as in the case of the Tonkin Gulf Resolution."

"As bad a bucking horse?"

"You know about that, Rachel?"

"You were, I understand, kicked in the head by a horse in 1951."

"I sustained major injuries. That damned kick nearly tore off my lips."

"Not a good thing for a senator."

"The kick also fractured my jaw in four places and knocked out most of my upper teeth."

"No fun."

"My political foes were not completely unhappy. Many of them considered me to be a "jackass."

"You can still laugh at yourself?"

"It helped me to get through the worst of days."

"I need to remember that. Now I have a question for you, Rachel. I'm told you'll meet with my buddy, Ernest. Perhaps you would share what you learned about his background."

"Sir, I met with him in his home in Anchorage, Alaska."

CHAPTER 31

THE NEW YORKER

"You've seen "old man Morse" before interviewing me?"

"I have, Mr. Gruening"

"Well, if you see him again tell him to keep fighting, Miss Bloom."

"Rachel, please."

"Fine. Where do we start?"

"Your New York City days?"

"I was born on February 6, 1887. My father was Emil Gruening. He was of German abstraction and an eye and ear surgeon. My mother was Phebe Frienberg, a well-educated woman. I was educated in fine public schools and then attended Harvard University. I graduated from the Harvard Medical School in 1912."

"But you didn't practice?"

"Very little. I gravitated toward journalism, which I found most exciting, if not challenging."

"In time you became the editor of *The Nation*, a fine progressive magazine."

"I also did a short stint as the editor of *The New York Post*."

"That was before you got involved with the FDR and his New Deal?"

"Quite a guy, Rachel."

"He got you involved with Alaska?"

"I was appointed to the Alaska International Highway Commission in 1938. In 1939 I was appointed Governor of Alaska, years before statehood. I would serve for 13 and half years."

"You were an outspoken advocated for Alaskan Statehood?"

"Absolutely."

"Your speech in 1955 stated the case?"

"I spoke before the Alaska Constitutional Convention, telling those there, 'Let us end American Colonialism.'"

"You equated the situation to Great Britain's Empire in North America before the Revolutionary War."

"I compared Alaska to our relationship with Cuba and Puerto Rico, and to the Philippines until independence was granted after WWII for that Asian country. I also stated, Rachel, that from the moment Alaska was purchased, there was an implied promise of statehood."

"All that came to pass in 1959?"

"Indeed."

"You then became one of the two inaugural senators?"

"It was my honor."

"Senator, I understand you are considered an expert on Mexico?"

"Some suggest that."

"Including the Government of Mexico, which award you the Order of the Aztec Eagle for your comprehensive book on the country?"

"Mexico City was kind enough to consider my work the best by a non-Mexican writer."

"Quite a honor."

"Rachel, isn't it time we moved on? Let's get to the real subject at hand."

"Tonkin Gulf?"

CHAPTER 32

THE TONKIN GULF RESOLUTION

After interviewing both senators, I pulled together their responses to President Johnson's Vietnam Policy. It is best to begin with the legal language presented to the Congress.

Section 1 – The Congress approves and supports the determination of the president, as Commander and Chief, to take all necessary measures to repeal any armed attack against the forces of the United States and to prevent further aggression.

Section 2 - The United States regards as vital to its national interests and to world peace the maintenance of international peace and security in Southeast Asia. The United States is, therefore, prepared as the President determines, to take all necessary steps including the use of armed forces, to assist any member or protocol state of the Southeast Asia Collective Defense Treaty (SEATO) requesting assistance in defe3nse of its freedom.

Section 3 – This resolution shall expire when the President shall determine that the peace and security of the area is reasonably assured by international conditions crated by action of the United

Nations or otherwise, except that it may be terminated earlier by concurrent resolution of the Congress.

The resolution sailed through the House of Representatives, 410 to 0. In the Senate the vote was 88 to 2.

PRESIDENT JOHNSON

The Senate was divided into three distinct groups. One group gave totally uncritical support to President Johnson. I asked Senator Gruening about that.

"To me that was irresponsible. Presidents can be wrong. Presidential egos can be troublesome. Running a war on the basis of polling can be dangerous. Presidents can be trapped by their own rhetoric and their desire to be loved and reelected."

A second group supported the president, but wanted a complete review of America's foreign policy after the conflict came to an end. I again asked the Senator for his thoughts.

"That all sounded nice, Rachel, but did it really mean? It meant, I thought at the time, to just shoving the problem down the road. Such thinking permitted the warhorse to gallop out of the barn. Trying to get him back in would be the problem. You're already at war. It seemed senseless to authorize war and later to review the policies that led to war."

"That sounds like something Senator Morse would say."

"Well, we were in agreement on that one. Anyway, a New Yorker can love horses, too."

"I share that thought with him."

"You do that, Rachel. Now what about the third group?"

The last group was unalterably opposed to the president's war resolution as written. Too much power, unlimited in actuality, was being given to the President. Though others may have supported this position, only two Senators voted with their feet.

"Morse."

"And you, Sir."

"How would you describe your reasoning for this view?"

"Our minority views can be summarized as follows:

"First, the US Navy provoked the North Vietnamese PT boat attack on the two American destroyers in the Gulf of Tonkin. The North claimed a 12-miles off shore boundary. International law said 3-miles. Regardless, the *C. Turner Joy* and the *USS Maddox* were in dangerous waters collecting intelligence information on the North's radar capabilities. The two warships should not have been there in the first place."

"You didn't believe the White House's account?"

"We wanted more details. We wanted to unseal the Navy's records of the incident."

"That never happened?"

"Only partially and most reluctantly."

————————

"Second, the attack was not premeditated by Hanoi. Therefore, it was not an act of war in the traditional sense. It was an incident, an unplanned engagement. The North could not have known in advance where two ships would be or even when. Had the attack been premeditated the damage to American ships would have, it is assumed, been greater. Given the sketchy reports from the Navy, and the unwillingness of the Administration to provide greater details, what transpired was open to debate. Did the actual engagement occur as the White House reported?

"You thought the President was skewing the information?"

"We, Morse and myself, wanted to look at all the intelligence information."

"The Administration declined."

"That's a kindly way of saying it."

————————

"Third, the US bombing on the North in retaliation for the attack had inflected enough damage. Understand that damage is not just blowing up physical structures. Civilians are killed. How many people had to die before our thirst for revenge was satiated? Remember, no sailor had been killed. There was no need for further escalation. There was no need for B-52's to be carpet bombing villages. How much was enough for the Administration? Was retaliation now a situation without restraint and was the President lurching purposely into a wider conflict? These were uncomfortable questions, but they needed to be asked at the time."

RETALIATION

———————

"Fourth, what was taking place in Vietnam was a civil war, not a war of northern aggression. That being the case the United States had no business getting involved. We should have heeded President Abraham Lincoln's admonishment to the British, French, and Spanish during our American Civil War. Lincoln stated in terms that could not be misunderstood that the conflict was a local affair and they (Europe) should not take sides. That was the advice we should have taken. If self-determination was a vital American policy, we should leave it to the people of Vietnam to determine their own fate."

"But the Chinese were assisting the North?"

"True, but not with troops."

"The Russians were also helping Ho Chi Minh?"

"Yes, but again not with troops on the ground."

"You wanted to play be their rules?"

"We didn't want American boys thrown into that tempest."

———————

"Fifth, the United States was violating the Geneva Accords of 1954. We were not honoring the Accords because, as the President stated, "hostile action was occurring in Vietnam that would threaten our allies in the region." A civil war was not a hostile action. In any event, the US had failed to support free and fair elections, which would have brought Ho Chi Minh to power. If the United States had adhered to the Geneva Accords no ships would have been attacked and no war resolution would have been needed."

"Our government opposed the elections?"

"Rachel that should be obvious. Washington was not about to let the Vietnamese people decide that they wanted a communist government controlling the country."

"If the South's leader had been more popular?"

"If Diem had an excellent chance of winning, only then would free elections have been held. But beyond Catholics and his urban base, he was unpopular. The peasant farmers in the rural villages were against him. Our government knew that. We were backing a loser."

––––––––––

Sixth, the United States, by its unilateral actions, was not using the good offices of the United Nations and a possible diplomatic resolution to the crisis. Specifically the United States had violated the UN Charter, Article 2, Section 4:

> All members shall refrain in international relationships from the use of force against the territorial integrity or political independence of any state or in any other manner inconsistent with the purpose of the UN.

Also, the United States had violated Article 37 of the Charter:

Should the parties to a dispute of the nature referred to in Article 33 fail to settle it by the means indicated in the article, they shall refer it to the Security Council.

The United States had not tried to resolve the questions through negotiations and diplomacy, including either mediation or arbitration. The US had failed to go before the Security Council. Another uncomfortable question emerges. Did the United States really want a negotiated peace, which of necessity would benefit both sides? Or was Vietnam merely a Cold War pawn in our relationships with the Soviet Union and China?

"Are you saying the United States bypassed the United Nations?"

"We implemented our Vietnam war policies unilaterally. We were not concerned about world opinion regardless of White House rhetoric to the contrary."

"And international law?"

"It was not a restraint."

———————

"Seventh, the Tonkin Gulf Resolution preempted the proper procedures to follow when American becomes involved in a war. The President hadn't asked Congress for a declaration of war as had Woodrow Wilson and FDR. The Tonkin Gulf Resolution essentially removed Congress from the process and gave too much power to the White House. The President could, if he wished, expand the war. Escalation was not only possible it was now probable. That was the only logical conclusion since the President now had a "blank check"

"This was where you and Morse drew a line?"

"In the sand as they say. We parted ways with President Johnson and Secretary of Defense McNamara."

THE SECRETARY OF DEFENSE

"Eighth, the Domino Theory was a house of cards. It did not take into consideration the history, culture, and vital interests of Laos, Cambodia, Thailand, India, or Burma. These countries were not dominos. They were not a monolithic body. All of them harbored a degree of fear concerning both China and Japan, and certainly they had no love of the British and French. A communist Vietnam did not mean Southeast Asia would fall under the sway of Moscow or China. While influenced by the Cold War, wars of national independence were nationalistic in nature as they brought an end to Western imperialism in the region. Unfortunately, Washington refused to accept this thesis whether out of ignorance or stubbornness."

"Johnson and his advisers didn't understand what was going on?

"One could make that argument."

"You and Morse did."

"We were replacing France with our occupying armies. It was a new form of imperialism no matter how the justifications for war were couched. We were not siding with a people seeking their independence. We wanted an outcome acceptable for maintaining the status quo in the Cold War. Our so-called revolutionary spirit was long gone."

––––––––––

"Senator Gruening, your response to the Tonkin Gulf Resolution was immediate and powerful."

> *I find myself in disagreement with the President's Southeast Asian policy… We are sending our boys into combat in a war in which we have no business, which is not our war, into which we have been misguidedly drawn, which is steadily being escalated. This resolution is a further authorization for escalation unlimited. I am opposed to sacrificing a single American boy in this venture. We have lost far too many already…*

"Senator Morse stated his views paralleling yours?"
"He did. He said:

> *I believe that history will record that we have made a great mistake in subverting and circumventing the Constitution of the United States… I believe this resolution to be a historic mistake. I believe that within the next century, future generations will look with dismay and great disappointment upon a Congress, which is now about to make such a historic mistake.*

"On March 10, 1964 you said you were "against the bloodshed, against the expense, against the number of refugees resulting from combat, and against how it had changed the world view on the morality of the United States."

"Those were my words.

"Later you said 'the US entrance into the Southeast Asian theatre was "misguided" and called for an apology by the Administration."

"Yes."

"You also pointed out the obvious: 'After you have been bombing villagers with napalm, it's going to be very difficult to persuade people that you are their friend.'"

"What else could we expect, Rachel?"

As I understand it, following the first "Teach-in Protest" in 1965 your colleague in dissent, Senator Morse, said, "It is urgent that the American people insist that their country return to a respect for law before we create a holocaust in Asia." He lavished praise for the student protesters who were willing to take a stand."

"Morse was eloquent in an Oregonian sort of way."

"He also said:

> Protest rallies… ought to be multiplied by the hundreds across America… The people want the facts and they want a justification, which they have not been getting, because all they have been getting is propaganda.
>
> The formulation of American foreign policy under the Constitution belongs to the people of the United States, not exclusively to the President and the State Department.

"All of which I agreed with, as you might expect. Youth needed to stop youth from being sent to the killing fields of Southeast Asia. The so-called adults in Washington were certainly not doing it."

"The students were ahead of their parents?"

"They were ahead of a lot of things."

"Senator Morse also pointed out, as I already had, that 'not one voice has yet answered his contention 'that the US, under the leadership of Defense Secretary McNamara, was fighting an illegal and unwise war in Vietnam.' He went on to say that 'the place to settle the controversy is not on the battlefield but around the conference table.'"

"Our government wasn't ready for that?"

"Sadly, no; guns and bombs before diplomacy was their answer. But some day…"

"Some day what?"

"All wars come to an end, and they end at the negotiating table to clean up the mess, one way or another. This business in Vietnam will be no different. It's just a matter of how many lives will be lost before the inevitable takes place?"

"Senator Gruening, you are cynical about this?"

"No, just realistic. It happened in Korea. It will happen in Vietnam. And sadly, beyond the present crisis, it will take place again in the next war. That's not cynicism. That's the lesson of history."

"Do we really learn the lessons of history, Sir?"

"Well, as President Lincoln said, 'you can take a horse to water, but you can't make him drink.' Old Morse knew that and left us with a warning as I recall.

> *There is no hope for permanent peace in the world until all nations of the world are willing to set up a system of international justice through law to which will be submitted each and every issue that threatens the peace of the world, for final and binding decision to be imposed by and an international organization as the United Nations.*

"In *The Nation* (May 5, 1969) you tried to put the Vietnam War into some kind of historic perspective: You wrote and I quote:

> *It is, and for some time has been, obvious that the most important issue facing our nation is to get out of the war in Southeast Asia. All our other issues and problems are slighted, impaired and unresolved until we halt the fighting, stop the continuing drain of blood and treasure, and turn to the long-neglected pressing needs at home.*

"You have quoted me correctly. There is little I can add."

"Then it is time for me to go."

"Write a good book, Rachel. Morse and the others deserve that."

"As does old Marty Cohen's sour stomach."

CHAPTER 33

RETHINKING – AUGUST 1975

I'm sitting alone now in my Seattle rental. My roommates are out on the town. They wanted me to come along. They had someone, as always, for me to meet. I guess I just wasn't in the mood. I've finished writing up my notes for Professor Simmons. I've done a good job. I had to. The men I interviewed deserved that and more. I'm sitting here alone with a glass of red wine thinking about those two old men. Who would have thought they would both die last year. On June 26, 1974 Ernest Gruening died in Washington D.C. He was 87-years old. On July 24, 1974 Wayne Morris passed away. He died in Good Samaritan Hospital in Portland of kidney failure. He was 73-years old.

I have to admit it. I'll miss them. I have another confession. I've come to like history and public servants who put principle before politics. So don't tell anyone, but I'm considering running for a local council spot in Seattle. I guess Wayne and Ernest got to me.

BOOK 3

THE MIDDLE EAST TINDERBOX

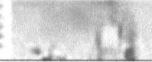

The day was Tuesday. The date was September 11, 2001. The location was New York City. It was early morning. Out of the apparently innocent sky two hijacked commercial airliners crashed into the Twin Towers of the World Trade Center. The first plane crashed at 8:46 am. Seventeen minutes later the second plane did so. The destruction was total. The coordinated attack was conducted by al-Qaeda, a militant Islamist terrorist group. A third plane crashed into the west side of the Pentagon in the suburbs of Washington D.C. The time was 9:37 am. The damage was extensive. A fourth plane plowed into a field near Shanksville, Pennsylvania. Its intended target was the White House or the US Capitol. The attacks resulted in 2,977 fatalities and over 25,000 injuries. The property damage exceeded $10 billion. It was the single most deadly terrorist attack in human history.

In response to the attack President George W. Bush launched what came to be known as a "War on Terror." This led to an invasion of Afghanistan to depose the Taliban government, which had not expelled al-Qaeda and its leader Osama bin Laden from the country before the attack as requested by Washington. Authorization for the invasion required approval by the US Congress. A Joint Resolution was submitted by the Bush Administration to Congress. It is often referred to as the AUMF --- Authorization for the use of military force. The salient passage was as follows:

> *The President is authorized to use all necessary and appropriate force against those nations, organizations, or persons he determines planned, authorized, committed, or aided the terrorist attacks that occurred on September 11, 2001, or harbored such organizations or persons, in order to prevent any future acts of international terrorism against the United States by such nations, organizations or persons.*

The US Senate passed the Joint Resolution by a vote of 98 to 0. The vote in the House of Representatives was 420 to 1. Representative Barbara Lee cast the solitary dissenting vote. This is her story.

PART VI
A SINGULAR VOICE

KIDS CAN'T SEE US BOMBING AND THEN LISTEN TO US TALKING ABOUT GETTING GUNS OUT THE SCHOOLS. HOW CAN WE TELL THEM TO SOLVE PRBLEMS WITHOUT VIOLENCE, IF IN FACT, WE CAN'T SHOW AN ABILITY TO SOLVE PROBLEMS WITHOUT VIOLENCE?

BARBARA LEE

CHAPTER 34

OAKLAND - 2003

The old Buick maneuvered through the dense early morning downtown traffic before entering the San Francisco Bay Bridge, which connected the "City of St. Francis" with its eastern neighbor, Oakland. As always, the four lanes traveling eastward were congested. The driver, a young woman, concentrated on steering safely across the span, yet she found herself thinking aloud about the appointment she was keeping. "She's finally agreed to see me. Who would have believed it?"

The question hung in the air, or in this case, high above the bay the first Spanish explorers thought could "house all the ships of the world." Below the great stretch of steel and cement was a cluster of container ships with products from throughout the world for COSTCO and Wal-Mart, and thousands of other much smaller stores. Elegant cruise ships also plied the waters below, some just arriving, others disembarking, all with generally happy passengers. Immense tankers, really floating gas stations bringing crude oil and natural gas from the Mideast, churned slowly through the waters. There would be no shortage of gasoline today. If the weather cooperated, and the winds were favorable, a myriad of small sailing boats would also dot the watery landscape below.

The young woman continued to muse as she exited the bridge at its eastern terminus. "She gave me directions to her home in the hills above the city. Now, assuming I don't get lost, I should arrive on time. That's important because she's a stickler for promptness, or so I've been told."

It took a few minutes for the young woman to arrive at her destination, but she was on time. It was exactly 8:46 am. "A strange time," she thought aloud as she parked. Carrying a large briefcase and her bulky old leather purse, she walked up to the front door and knocked. A moment later the door opened to reveal a beautiful black woman of indefinite middle age.

"Miss Arlene Bloom?"
"Mrs. Barbara Lee?"

The young woman was ushered into the spacious house and then into a lovely room with a large French window that provided a magnificent view of the Bay Bridge and in the distance, the skyscrapers of the City.

"Well, Miss Bloom, we meet at last."
"Arlene, please."
"You are a persistent one."
"A trait I inherited from my mother."
"Rachel Bloom?"
"Yes."
"It's an admirable trait for a women."
"Especially in Congress, I would assume?"
"Exceedingly so.
"Mrs. Lee, I appreciate you meeting with me."

"Barbara will be fine. Now as to why I consented… Beyond your letters and phone calls, you sent me a box of materials, including the book co-authored by Mr. Simmons and your mother."

"I hoped they might influence you to see me, Barbara."

"They did. I must admit I knew nothing about this elusive character Marty Cohen, though I was, as you might imagine, aware of the dissenters this died in the wool Socialist interviewed."

"Secretary of State William Jennings Bryan?"

"Yes, and Senators Norris and LaFollette?"

"And the special lady, Miss Rankin?"

"Speaking as a woman, especially her. What a brave soul, standing alone. Such a contrarian."

"Like you, Barbara?"

"At times, yes."

"You knew about Senator Ernest Gruening of Alaska?"

"Of course, Arlene."

"And Wayne Morris of Oregon?"

"A very special person. Your mother's interviews with the senators were most telling. All of them had one thing in common. They did not want to subvert or circumvent the Constitution. They did not want to give any president a "blank check" when it came to war powers. They always prized diplomacy over the use of military force. Those folks and their views preoccupied my mind when President Bush sought his War Resolution following the attack on the Twin Towers."

"And you've read the book, *Dissenters, Each and Every One*?"

"As I said, I did. What Simmons and your mother wrote weighed heavily on me as you might assume when I cast my recent vote. And that's why you're here, isn't it?"

"And, Barbara, that's why you wanted me here at this precise time, 8:46 a.m.?"

"I still feel unnerved when my watch seems to stop at that very moment."

"Difficult to believe what took place?"

"Not if you were there, Arlene, not if you saw the smoke and heard the sirens, and watched terrified people running from the Congressional Offices."

"I was away at Stanford doing research."

"I was at ground zero."

The two women paused. They needed to. They needed time to collect their thoughts. Then Mrs. Lee spoke.

"You're here to carry on for your mother?"

"I am. She passed a year ago. I'm trying to write a sequel to her work."

"Focusing on?"

"Dissenting women in Congress, beginning with you."

"I'm flattered, but why me?"

"It's simple: 420 to 1."

CHAPTER 35

STREET TOUGH

The two women were sipping tea and enjoying a delightful, if not sinful, very frosted bear claw.

"May we begin with your background, Barbara?"

"My years before I entered politics?"

"Yes."

"Some parts of my life were painful. I required that you be circumspect in what you write."

"Of course."

————————

"I was born in El Paso, Texas, July 16, 1946. My maiden name was Barbara Jean Tutt. I was the daughter of Mildred Adaire and Garvin Alexander Tutt. I am African-American. I can trace my ancestral line back to Sierra Leone, on the west coast of Africa. My father was a combat veteran. He served in World War II and Korea."

"Your early schooling, Barbara?"

"The schools in El Paso were segregated. My parents enrolled me in a Catholic school. I was the only black kid in the school."

"Eventually my parents moved to Los Angeles where I attended San Fernando High School in Pacoima, a sort of suburb of Los Angeles. I graduated in 1964. "

"That's when you became aware of racial issues?"

"Our school was racially mixed, but in an unusual way. If you were in a helicopter high above the school in the morning, you would have seen three groups of students streaming toward the school. Hispanics came in one direction. Blacks from another... Whites from still a third location. All met in the school yard."

"As you say, a racially mixed school."

"But not all treated in the same manner, Arlene. Our history books and my teachers, for example, glossed over the horrors of slavery I had to learn about my ancestors from other sources. That's when I learned about my great-grandmother who was a slave. Her owner, a terrible man, raped her numerous times. She bore several light-colored children."

"You think of her often?"

"I do. It's heart wrenching to think of the fear and pain she went through by this violent, predatory bigot."

"Tell me about the cheerleading incident?"

"You've been checking up on me, my high school years."

"A little, Barbara."

"I went out for the cheerleading team. There had never been a black on the team before, possibly a Hispanic. You had to be blonde, blue-eyed, and look the part whatever that meant. I wasn't blond, nor did I have blue eyes, but I could move. I was very athletic. I could do cheers and cartwheels. I finally earned a spot on the team. Not everyone was happy about that. I had to deal with some abuse in the hallways. This is what I looked like so long ago.

The older woman handed Arlene an old photograph.

CHEERLEADING

"Wow, pretty hot stuff."

"With lots of hair."

"What did you learn from this experience?"

"You have to fight for what you want. You have to be street tough if you want to succeed."

"Then you turned 16 and things got out of hand?"

"We must go into that?"

"That's up to you."

"I got pregnant. My Catholic education lacked teachings about contraception. I got married in secret and then I had a miscarriage. I followed my husband to England. He was in the Air Force. We had two sons. At age 20 I got divorced. At the time I was homeless and without a job. I had to go on welfare."

"You take responsibility for your predicament?"

"I do, but also for what happened later."

"You went back to school?"

"I received federal assistance to attend Mills College in Oakland. I couldn't afford childcare. I dragged my two boys to classes with me. I hauled them everywhere. It wasn't easy."

"But there was no choice?"

"As you say, Arlene, there was no choice."

"You then got your MA degree in social work at the University of California, Berkeley."

"Still dragging my boys, I did in 1973."

"And then politics beckoned."

"Yes, but before we proceed. That federal assistance made all the difference in my life. That's why I'm a firm supporter of such programs. They provide opportunity. They provide hope. Include that message in your book."

"Of course."

———————

"I became active in the failed presidential campaign of a special woman, Shirley Chisholm. She was a Democrat and the first black woman to seek a major party's nomination. Her fighting slogan was "unbought and unbossed.""

"Words that you adopted in your political career?"

"If you are to keep your promises to the voters and be true to your convictions, yes. Her words were inspiring."

"Of course, she had no hope of winning the nomination, but she had put a foot in the door."

A BLACK CANDIDATE

"You then went to work for Representative Ron Dellums."

"Yes. We had much in common. He was also a social worker. He had served in the Marine Corps and that, of course, reminded me of my father. I worked myself up through the ranks in Dellums' office. He supported all along. He was a great mentor."

"He imparted his political wisdom?"

"He did. We talked about the emotional state of the country and how to make rational decisions even under the most difficult of situations. He told me to never make a decision in the heat of emotion or in fear. Why? Because, as he said, you'll probably make the wrong decision 'if you're doing stuff based on fear.'"

"When he retired, you won his seat in a special election?"

"I did. That was in 1998."

"I understand he spoke to you before your dissenting vote? Do you recall what he said?"

RON DELLUMS

"He didn't tell me how to vote. He simply asked me to consider the implications of my vote. He reminded me to not be poll-driven in my actions."

"He eventually retired from Congress in 1997?"

"That is correct. A special election was held to fill his position in the 9th Congressional District. I entered the race and won."

"You were now off to Washington?"

"Where election after election I have remained."

"Shall we turn to September 11th?"

CHAPTER 36

THAT TERRIBLE DAY

"Where were you on that day?"

"I was attending a meeting with a representative of the Small Business Administration. You know, just another meeting. I was there with several members of the Congressional Black Caucus. We wanted the agency to increase support to black businesses. Suddenly I heard the Capital Police yelling, 'Get out of the building. Now!' We did."

"You didn't know what had happened?"

"At that moment, no. And once on the street I didn't know which way to run, even where to go. An officer just pointed down the street. I ran. I was running toward the Supreme Court. I was on Pennsylvania Avenue. I looked around. All I saw was smoke, ugly and frightening. I didn't know it was coming from the Pentagon."

"Were you in shock?"

"Not in the usual sense in terms of how I felt. Scared, yes. Paralyzed, no... I was still street smart, though a little older. I was shocked when I found out what had really occurred. In time I would feel the pain that my constituents felt and the harm done to so many people."

"You went to the memorial service?"

"Yes, it was held in the Washington National Cathedral three days later. Reverend Nathan Baxter spoke and I took his words to heart.

Let us also pray for divine wisdom as our leaders consider the necessary actions for national security, wisdom of the grace of God, that as we act we not become the evil we deplore.

"You used his words in your speech of dissent?"

"They seemed most appropriate."

"Did you expect the Bush Administration to act so quickly with the request to use military force?"

"I knew some sort of War Resolution would be forthcoming from the White House. I knew it would be popular. People were upset. They were angry. They tasted blood and wanted revenge. I was not oblivious to all that. Indeed, I also wanted justice. I wanted al-Qaeda stopped. I wanted Osama bin Laden behind bars. What he had done was evil. He needed to pay a price."

THE PERPETRATOR

"So you weren't surprised?"

"I've come to believe Bush's team had something in the works well before September 11th."

"Like Wilson, FDR, and President Johnson?"

"One could make that argument."

"They were already preparing for war?"

"Among other options, yes."

The two women paused again. It was as if they were considering the polar opposite possibilities always open to a president, war or peace, threats or diplomacy, rattling the sword or sitting at the negotiating table.

"You were already considering how you would vote if President George Bush wanted a War Resolution?"

"It was on my mind. I needed to see the exact language. I needed to consider the implications if the Congress passed such a resolution. Though some might argue I was premature in my thinking, I did have questions.

1. Would the War Resolution name the specific country to be attacked?
2. Would the document list where else force would be authorized?
3. Would the mission objectives be spelled out?
4. Would our actions be in compliance with accepted International Law?
5. Would there be clear reporting to the American people about the mission?
6. Would there be an expiration date?"

"Lots of questions?"

"The same questions that troubled Miss Rankin and the others. I was not, as you can assume, immune to them. I was concerned, as they had been, that the country not embarks on an open-ended war with neither an exit strategy nor a focused target. If we went to war, I didn't want our country to repeat past mistakes."

"You were mindful of Miss Rankin?"

"Not completely. She was a pacifist. I was not. If military action were necessary I would support it. I was against a 'blank check,' so broad in scope that a president could do almost anything he wanted. If it came to it I wanted a resolution that didn't give away Congress's constitutional requirements to declare war or to authorize the use of force. My moral compass and my faith wanted to find solutions short of an all-out war. One thing was for sure. I didn't want to give President Bush or any occupant of the White House virtually unlimited power to declare and wage war against an enemy defined only as 'terrorism.' The Constitution required me to vote in time, but it didn't dictate how I should vote."

"Let's now turn to your vote."

"It was my turn to respond to the White House."

PRESIDENT BUSH

CHAPTER 37

THE VOTE

SEPTEMBER 14, 2001

"I rose and voted no. It was as simple as that, at least on the surface. I had, of course, my reasons."

"Reasons that were at first dismissed by many."

"The immediate public response outside of my Congressional District was not favorable. Almost immediately I started receiving death threats. The Capitol Police provided me with around the clock security. Officers shadowed me when I went grocery shopping, even when I went to church. People called me all times of the day and night. They were not friendly calls. My children were threatened. People called me a traitor. I was called racist and sexist names. One person compared me to a dog. But not even an American dog; I was a black mutt."

"The price of dissent?"

"Always expensive. The *Washington Times* called me "a long practicing supporter of America's enemies." The *Wall Street Journal* described me as a 'clueless liberal' and asked if I was 'anti-American?'" During a Veterans Day Parade a political rival said, 'Barbara Lee hates America. He had a poster showing my face smiling in front of the burning World Trade Towers."

"That's crazy."

"Arlene, that was just the beginning. One individual wrote:

> *Regarding your lone dissent; the terrorists used God as an excuse. Is it true God helped you make your decision too? Congratulations on using terrorist mentality.*

Another person wrote me:

> *Did you hope to go down as the sole pacifist in a sea of war-mongers? If so, you missed the mark. You will go down in history as the sole coward in a sea of courageous legislators.*

"Your father called you?"

"Yes. He was 77 at the time. He said 'it was the right vote.' He reminded me to never do anything that was irrational --- that we had to be thoughtful and understand the implications of our actions.'"

"Which is what you tried to do."

"That about sums it up, Arlene."

"Your constituents?"

"They reelected me with 82% of the votes. At least in my Congressional District, I felt vindicated."

"You did try to explain yourself?"

"I put out a printed statement. In the heat of the moment few paid attention to it.

"Perhaps we can go into it, point by point?"

_____

"I began by saying I had a heavy heart for the families and loved ones who were killed and injured. I understood the grief of the American people. The unspeakable attack has forced me to rely on my moral compass, my conscience, and my God for direction."

"Then you got to the key point?"

"September 11th changed the whole world. However, I am unconvinced that military action will prevent further acts of international terrorism against the United States."

"Your colleagues didn't agree?"

"Or if they did, they muted that view out of a pragmatic necessity to be reelected."

"You went on?"

"The War Resolution will pass, I wrote. I knew that. The president will have power to make war. I simply want to urge restraint. We must think through the implications of what we're about to do. We must look to and understand the consequences of our actions."

"Few wanted to do that, Barbara?"

"War fever was in the air as it was in 1917, after Pearl Harbor, during the Vietnam War, and now after the Twin Towers were bombed."

"You then provided your own take on the situation."

"I did, Arlene. I said we are not dealing with a conventional war. Therefore, we cannot respond in a conventional manner. The current crisis, I pointed out, requires a multi-faceted approach since it involves national security, foreign policy, public safety, intelligence gathering, and outright murder. I then added what many people found objectionable:

> We must not rush to judgment. Far too many innocent people have already died. Our country is in mourning. If we rush to launch counter-attack, we run too great a risk that women, children, and other non-combatants will be caught in the crossfire.

"And then you got into really hot water?"

"I said:

Nor can we let our justified anger over these outrageous acts by vicious murderers inflame prejudice against all Arab Americans, Muslims, Southeast Asians, or any other people because of their race, religion, or ethnicity.

"A difficult thing to ask Americans while the smoke was still billowing in New York and bodies were still being unearthed in the debris."

"Unfortunately, that was the case."

"Still, you had to try?"

"I recalled President Johnson's request to 'take all necessary measures to repel attacks and prevent further aggression.' That led to escalation and to a decade of war. At the time the House had abandoned its own constitutional responsibilities and launched our nation into years of an undeclared war. I did not want to see that happen again."

"History repeating itself?"

"Yes. I ended my statement, as I had when I cast my vote. I quoted what I had heard at the Memorial Service:

As we act, let us not become the evil that we deplore.

———————

There was little to say at this point. The two women knew that.

"You'll write a good book. I'll expect a copy."

"The first copy off the press will be for you, Barbara, as will the first chapter."

CHAPTER 38

A LEGACY OF COURAGE

Congresswoman Barbara Lee still represents her Oakland community in the 13th Congressional District. She is 76-years of age and continues to fight for a progressive agenda and for the repeal of the Authorization for Use of Military Force Against Terrorists (AUMF). The House has approved of her efforts to do so, but the legislation always stalls in the Senate. What keeps her going is the desire to "restore the balance to this Constitution" when it comes to war powers. Lawmakers have been unable to agree on key details in reforming or replacing the current law. Three questions continue to stymie the Senate; First, how long should any authorization last? Second, what countries should it be applied to? Third, would changes allow for the use of American ground forces? Though the questions are difficult to resolve Barbara Lee perseveres.

In supporting Barbara Lee's reelection campaigns, Congressman John Lewis said of her:

Representative Barbara Lee has been a tireless fighter for justice, civil rights, and equality and an outspoken advocate for the most vulnerable in our society. Across her years of service, Representative Lee has worked to uplift, not only the

Congressional Black Caucus, but also to bring together members of our party from diverse backgrounds.

Somewhere in the skies above Jeannette Rankin and others must be smiling. And, if we look closely, quite possibly we'll catch a glimpse of old Marty Cohen questioning still another politician, even as he complains of a sour stomach.

EPILOGUE

They are all gone now, all but one, Barbara Lee. The others find residence in the quiet pages of history. Their thoughts and deeds live on for those who care to peel back the years and to once again hear their persistent voices filling the political air of the House and Senate with a dissenting vote to, if at all possible, avoid war. Much has been written about these contrarians and perhaps more will be said in the future. For now, as we bid them farewell, we will, as we should, let them speak in their own words, and from what they say, we can derive some understanding of their times and our own days.

We will begin with William Jennings Bryan, a principled public servant who relinquished his Cabinet position as Secretary of State under President Woodrow Wilson.

> *Destiny is no matter of chance. It is a matter of choice. It is not a thing to be waited for; it is thing to be achieved.*

> *My place in history will depend on what I can do for the people and not on what the people can do for me.*

> *Facts mean nothing unless they are rightly understood, rightly related, and rightly interpreted.*

Robert LaFollette's call to battle on behalf of the common man still resonates in the Senate, unrelenting and undaunted by those prepared to go to war or resistant to ending social injustice.

Let no man think we can deny civil liberty to others and retain it for ourselves. When zealous agents of the Government arrest suspected "radicals" without warrant, hold them without prompt bail, deny them access to counsel and admission of bail... we have shorn the Bill of Rights of its sanctity. Democracy is a life, and involves continual struggle.

For thirty years George W. Norris went about his business in the Senate, quietly and persistently advocating for the peaceful resolution of problems, whether domestic or foreign.

During practically all of my public life, I have been a sincere advocate of an agreement between the leading nations of the world to set up all the necessary international machinery that would bring about a practical abolition of war between civilized nations. There is not much danger of the smaller nations if the big nations will behave. Men are often biased in their judgment on account of their sympathy and their interests.

Jeannette Rankin's career in government was short lived, but not without import. As the first woman elected to the US Congress she paved the way for all those who followed her. Her willingness to be a dissenting voice against war marked her hours in the public forum.

> *You can no more win a war than you can win an earthquake.*
>
> *The individual woman is required... a thousand times a day to choose either to accept her appointed role and thereby rescue her good disposition out of the wreckage of her self-respect, or else follow an independent line of behavior and rescue her self-respect out of the wreckage of her good disposition.*
>
> *I worked for suffrage for years, and got it. I've worked for peace for 55 years and haven't come close.*
>
> *If I had my life to live over, I would do it all again, but this time I would be nastier.*

———————

Ernes Gruening vote in the Senate against the Tonkin Gulf Resolution exhibited the fierce independence of thinking often associated with Alaskans. Regardless of conventional political realities, he was always his own man, and always satisfied, if necessary, to be in the minority. He spoke out against the Vietnam War in the strongest terms long before other liberals were willing to do so. In doing so he showed extraordinary political courage. It was not easy. As he said:

> *Leaders often find themselves temporarily alone.*

———————

Senator Wayne Morse was loved by some and despised by others, but he could never be ignored. Much like his counterpart from

Alaska, this Oregonian was fiercely independent and always true to his convictions.

> *"I consider every additional life that is sacrificed in this forlorn venture a tragedy. Some day...if this sacrificing is continued it will be denounced as a crime.*
>
> *The only hope of advancing the cause of peace in our time lies in the substitution of the rules of international law for the jungle law of military might.*
>
> *I would be glad to walk out of the Senate if staying there meant I must vote to continue American outlawry in Southeast Asia.*
>
> *Don't send me back to Washington unless you want me to sit in the Senate as a free man --- free to vote in the public interest as the facts and my conscience dictate.*

Barbara Lee continues her work in the House of Representatives. She is still a strong liberal voice for those seeking social justice and an alternative to war. Those who have already departed are friendly shadows as she speaks today.

> *I wish the press were paying more attention to the erosion of the Constitution and the slippery slope that we're getting into, by giving up the right of the Congress to talk about when and how and where we go to war.*
>
> *I think that there's going to be a rush to judgment on civil liberties, and a clamping down, a suspension of our democratic rights. And I believe that those who are good Americans would want to see this not happen and that we debate how to find*

a balance between the public safety and the protection of civil liberties.

————————————

Our story now comes to an end. We are left at least with two questions. What lessons can be drawn from the political lives of these seven people, and how, given the difficult days we're passing through today, can we give perspective to their dissenting votes? In his book, *Profiles in Courage,* John Kennedy --- our martyred president --- provided a possible answer.

Politics merely furnishes one arena, which imposes special tests of courage. In whatever arena of life one may meet the challenge of courage, whatever may be the sacrifices he faces if he follows his conscience --- the loss of his friends, his fortune, his contentment, even the esteem of his fellow men --- each man must decide for himself the course he will follow.

www.ingramcontent.com/pod-product-compliance
Lightning Source LLC
Chambersburg PA
CBHW021619120626
46545CB00001B/305